THE FRANKFURT SCHOOL

KEY SOCIOLOGISTS
Series Editor: Peter Hamilton
The Open University

KEY SOCIOLOGISTS

Series Editor: PETER HAMILTON
The Open University, Milton Keynes

This series will present concise and readable texts covering the work, life and influence of many of the most important sociologists, and sociologically-relevant thinkers, from the birth of the discipline to the present day. Aimed primarily at the undergraduate, the books will also be useful to pre-university students and others who are interested in the main ideas of sociology's major thinkers.

MARX and Marxism
PETER WORSLEY, Professor of Sociology, University of Manchester

MAX WEBER
FRANK PARKIN, Tutor in Politics and Fellow of Magdalen College, Oxford

EMILE DURKHEIM
KENNETH THOMPSON, Reader in Sociology, Faculty of Social Sciences, The Open University, Milton Keynes

TALCOTT PARSONS
PETER HAMILTON, The Open University, Milton Keynes

SIGMUND FREUD
ROBERT BOCOCK, The Open University, Milton Keynes

C. WRIGHT MILLS
J. E. T. ELDRIDGE, Department of Sociology, University of Glasgow

THE FRANKFURT SCHOOL
TOM BOTTOMORE, Professor of Sociology, University of Sussex

GEORG SIMMEL
DAVID FRISBY, Department of Sociology, The University, Glasgow

KARL MANNHEIM
DAVID KETTLER, Professor of Political Studies, Trent University, Ontario, Canada
VOLKER MEJA, Associate Professor of Sociology, Memorial University of Newfoundland, and
NICO STEHR, Professor of Sociology, University of Alberta

THE FRANKFURT SCHOOL

TOM BOTTOMORE
Professor of Sociology
University of Sussex

R

ROUTLEDGE
London and New York

First published in 1984 by Ellis Horwood Ltd
and Tavistock Publications Ltd

Reprinted 1989 by Routledge
11 New Fetter Lane, London EC4P 4EE
29 West 35th Street, New York, NY 10001

Printed in Great Britain by
Richard Clay Ltd, Bungay, Suffolk

British Library Cataloguing in Publication Data
Bottomore, Tom
The Frankfurt School
1. Frankfurt school of sociology
I. Title   II. Series
301′.01 HM24
Library of Congress Card No. 84-551

ISBN 0-415-04279-8

Table of Contents

TOM BOTTOMORE is Professor of Sociology in the University of Sussex, Brighton. He joined the University in 1968, having been Professor and Head of the Department of Political Science, Sociology and Anthropology at the Simon Fraser University in Vancouver, since 1965. He is a graduate of the University of London with a B.Sc. in Economics (1943) and M.Sc. in Sociology (1949).

Professor Bottomore was President of the British Sociological Association (1969-1971); President of the International Sociological Association (1974-1978); and author of numerous previous books including *Political Sociology* (1979) and *Sociology and Socialism* (1984).

Editor's Foreword

The Frankfurt School of German social theory has exerted a considerable influence over the sociology of the last two generations. Originally a centre for the study of Marxist theory brought into being in the first years of Weimar Republic Germany, the work of its principal figures has nonetheless always had a somewhat ambiguous relationship with mainstream Western Marxism, right through from the early writings of Max Horkheimer in the 1930s to the very recent work of Jürgen Habermas. However, the development of a distinct 'critical theory' of society by Horkheimer and Adorno and its reworking by later Frankfurt theorists constituted a (sometimes tenuous) thread of ideas and concepts which gave the Frankfurt School an important role in the expansion of modern sociology. Despite the somewhat paradoxical rejection of Marxist concepts by many Frankfurt School writers, it was especially instrumental in the renaissance of Marxist sociology which took hold in the late 1960s.

Having remarked the gulf which separates much Frankfurt School work from mainstream Marxist theory, it is also interesting to note the striking parallels between the deep cultural pessimism of Max Weber's sociology—especially in its treatment of the rationalization processes of modern societies—and the thoroughgoing critique of bourgeois culture and intellectual thought developed by Horkheimer, Adorno and Marcuse as the main element of critical theory from the 1930s to the 1960s. As Tom Bottomore makes clear in drawing this parallel, the Frankfurt School thinkers were led by their pessimism into a retreat from Marxian social theory, and then towards an essentially philosophical and neo-Hegelian critique of ideology. Perhaps best seen as 'radicals in despair', Horkheimer, Marcuse and Adorno were responsible for a theory of capitalist society which emphasized its cultural manifestations above all other aspects. Caught in a climate of cultural loss and decline which must be linked to their experience of the rise of Fascism in Germany, the 'critical theory' developed by these men during this period was overwhelmingly concerned with the mounting irrationality of social and cultural values, and their reflection in the ideas of positivism and 'scientism'. Herbert Marcuse's version of 'critical theory' shares many of these aspects of *Ideologiekritik* conducted not from empirical observation but philosophical speculation, despite the fact that he preferred to stay on in the USA after the School returned from exile there in 1950, and was thus open to the influence of the strong empirical traditions of American social thought. His *One-Dimensional Man* (certainly his best known work) thus remains firmly within the contemplative cast of Frankfurt School work, its nature as a *philosophical* critique of advanced capitalism perhaps explaining why its great popularity did not lead to any significant attempts at extension or empirical demonstration of the thesis which it contains.

If Tom Bottomore's book gives the impression that the work of the Frankfurt School theorists has been largely sterile – for both Marxism *and* sociology – it also indicates some of the reasons why ideas which have received so much scholarly attention fall short of their promise. Indeed, it is of some significance that there has been such widespread interest in the ideas of the principal Frankfurt School theorists, for their work clearly struck a chord at a time when 'philosophical' interpretations of Marxist concepts were at the height of their popularity. It is not accidental that interest in the work of the School 'took off' – for want of a better word – after 1968 in the English-speaking world. The promise of an 'intellectualized' and culturally sophisticated quasi-Marxism had undeniable appeal.

But if Frankfurt School 'critical theory' has come to appear as a form of social theory more and more separate from Marxism since the 1960s, this is in part because of a return to structuralist and historical conceptions of Marxian theory themselves formulated to counter the excessively philosophical tenor of critical theory. With that process, as Tom Bottomore shows in this masterful book, went an increasing tendency for younger critical theorists such as Habermas to situate their work explicitly between philosophy and sociology. Whether such a strategy could ever be effective is open to question, especially since it has not implied any greater attention being paid to historical processes or to the empirical test of critical theory's tenets.

Tom Bottomore provides us in this book with a strikingly effective summary of the main features of the rise and decline of the Frankfurt School. This is a critical evaluation of the contributions of the main protagonists of 'critical theory', and its conclusions will in some ways be controversial. But in situating the failure of the Frankfurt School to generate a coherent paradigm of Marxist social theory in the refusal of its main figures to reach down from the high plane of philosophical contemplation to the murky waters of history and empirical facts, Tom Bottomore has undeniably touched the core of the matter.

Peter Hamilton

Introduction

The Frankfurt School is a complex phenomenon, and the style of social thought which has come to be principally associated with it – 'critical theory' – has been expounded and interpreted in a variety of ways. The institutional basis upon which the school developed was the Institute of Social Research, officially established on 3 February 1923 by a decree of the Ministry of Education, and affiliated with the University of Frankfurt. But the Institute itself was only the major, enduring outcome of several radical projects undertaken in the early 1920s by Felix Weil, the son of a wealthy grain merchant. Thus, in the summer of 1922 he had organized the 'First Marxist Work Week', attended among others by Lukács, Korsch, Pollock and Wittfogel, where much of the discussion was devoted to Korsch's forthcoming book, *Marxism and Philosophy*. Weil had intended to arrange further meetings of this kind, but when the idea of creating a more permanent centre of Marxist studies emerged he redirected his efforts and his financial resources to this project.[1]

The founding of the Institute took place in the particular conditions produced by the victory of the Bolshevik revolution in Russia and the defeat of the Central European revolutions, notably that in Germany; and it can be seen as one response to the need felt by left wing intellectuals to reappraise Marxist theory, and especially the relation between theory and practice, in the new circumstances. In this sense the Institute formed part of a wider movement of thought which has come to be known as 'Western Marxism', characterized on one side by diverse, predominantly philosophical and Hegelian reinterpretations of Marxist theory in relation to the advanced capitalist societies, and on the other, by an increasingly critical view of the development of society and the state in the USSR.[2] However, in its early phase the Institute did not constitute a distinctive school; as Jay has noted: '. . . the notion of a specific school did not develop until *after* the Institut was forced to leave Frankfurt (the term itself was not used until the Institut returned to Germany in 1950)'.[3]

In effect, it is possible to distinguish four distinct periods in the history of the Institute and the Frankfurt School. The first is that between 1923 and 1933, when the research carried on at the Institute was quite varied, and was in no way inspired by a particular conception of Marxist thought such as became embodied later in critical theory. Indeed, under its first Director, Carl Grünberg, who was an economic and social historian, closely related in outlook to the Austro-Marxists,[4] a considerable part of the Institute's work had a strongly empirical character. Grünberg himself summed up his conception of Marxism as a social science in his inaugural address (1924), in which he argued that 'the materialist conception of history neither is, nor aims to be, a philosophical system . . . its object is not abstractions, but the given concrete world in its process of development and change'. Under Grünberg's directorship, until his retirement in 1929 following a stroke, this was indeed the course taken by many of the Institute's researchers; thus Wittfogel was engaged in his study of the Asiatic mode of production (a part of which was published in 1931 as *Economy and Society in China*), Grossman developed his analysis of the economic tendencies of capitalism, published as *The Law of Accumulation and Collapse in the Capitalist System* (1929), and Pollock undertook a study of the transition from a market to a planned economy in the Soviet Union, *Experiments in Economic Planning in the Soviet Union, 1917–1927* (1929).

The second period is that of exile in North America from 1933 to 1950, when the distinctive ideas of a neo-Hegelian critical theory were firmly implanted as the guiding principle of the Institute's activities. This reorientation of ideas and research interests actually began a few years earlier, influenced particularly by the appointment of Horkheimer as director of the Institute in July 1930. As Jay has noted, with reference to Horkheimer's inaugural address on 'The Current Condition of Social Philosophy and the Tasks of an

Institute of Social Research' (1931), '. . . the differences between his approach and that of his predecessor were immediately apparent'.[5] Philosophy, rather than history or economics, now came to occupy a pre-eminent place in the Institute's work, and this tendency was reinforced when Marcuse became a member in 1932 and Adorno in 1938 (following a looser association with the Institute since 1931). At the same time the Institute developed a strong interest in psychoanalysis,[6] and this remained a prominent element in its later work. In exile the leading members of the Institute, under Horkheimer's direction, began to elaborate their theoretical views in a more systematic way, and a distinctive school of thought gradually took shape.

By the time the Institute returned to Frankfurt in 1950 the principal ideas of 'critical theory' had been clearly set out in a number of major writings, and the 'Frankfurt School' began to exert an important influence upon German social thought. Its influence later spread throughout much of Europe – especially after 1956, with the emergence of the 'New Left' – and also in the United States where many of the Institute's members (in particular Marcuse) had remained. This was the period of the Frankfurt School's greatest intellectual and political influence, which reached its peak in the late 1960s with the rapid growth of a radical student movement, though it was Marcuse rather than Horkheimer (who had by then retired to Switzerland) or Adorno (who had become considerably less radical during his exile in North America and in the changed circumstances of postwar Germany) who then appeared as the leading representative of a new form of Marxist critical thought.

From the early 1970s, in what can be regarded as its fourth period, the influence of the Frankfurt School slowly declined, and indeed with the death of Adorno in 1969 and of Horkheimer in 1973 it had virtually ceased to exist as a school. In its last years it had departed so widely from the Marxism which originally inspired it that in Jay's words '. . . it forfeited the right to be included among its many offshoots',[7] and its whole approach to social theory was increasingly contested by new, or revived forms of Marxist thought. Nevertheless, some of the central conceptions of the Frankfurt School have made their way into the work of many social scientists (both Marxist and non-Marxist), and they have also been developed in an original way by Jürgen Habermas, in a renewed critique of the conditions of possibility of social knowledge, and in reappraisals of Marx's theory of history and of modern capitalism.

In the following chapters I shall be concerned with the last three of the four periods I have distinguished, examining first the body of ideas which originally constituted the Frankfurt School, then the development and diffusion of those ideas in the school's heyday, and lastly the fate of the ideas in the post-Frankfurt era. This leads to some concluding reflections on the significance of the Frankfurt School, and its derivatives, for the sociological theory of the present time, and on its relation to any conceivable Marxist sociology in the future.

NOTES

[1] For a fuller account of the founding of the Institute, see Martin Jay, *The Dialectical Imagination* (Boston, Little, Brown & Co., 1973), chap. 1.

[2] 'Western Marxism' has generally been treated as a body of thought emerging in the 1920s and having its greatest influence in the 1960s, which had its source in the writings of Korsch, Lukács, Gramsci and some members of the Frankfurt Institute (in particular, from 1950 onwards, Horkheimer, Adorno and Marcuse). See, for varying interpretations of it, Andrew Arato and Paul Breines, *The Young Lukács and the Origins of Western Marxism* (New York, Seabury Press, 1979); and Perry Anderson, *Considerations on Western Marxism* (London, New Left Books, 1976). More comprehensively regarded, however, Western Marxism includes other, very different, forms of Marxist thought, and notably that of the Austro-Marxist School, which flourished from the turn of the century until 1934 and has recently attracted renewed attention. See Tom Bottomore and Patrick Goode (eds), *Austro-Marxism* (Oxford, Oxford University Press, 1978), Introduction.

[3] Jay, *op. cit.*, p. xv.

[4] For a brief account of Grünberg, see Bottomore and Goode, *op. cit.*, Introduction, pp. 9–10.

[5] Jay, *op. cit.*, p. 25.

[6] Thus Erich Fromm became a close collaborator in the early 1930s, but his increasingly critical view of Freudian theory, and his attempt to give psychoanalysis a more sociological dimension, led to disagreements, and he severed his connection with the Institute in 1939.

[7] Jay, *op. cit.*, p. 296.

1

The Formation of the School

Horkheimer, in the address delivered on the occasion of his official installation as director of the Institute in January 1931, indicated clearly, while paying tribute to the work of his predecessor, that the Institute was about to take a new direction. 'Social philosophy' now emerged as its main preoccupation; not in the sense of a philosophical theory of value which would provide a superior insight into the meaning of social life, nor as some kind of synthesis of the results of the specialized social sciences, but rather as the source of important questions to be investigated by these sciences and as a framework in which 'the universal would not be lost sight of'.[1] In subsequent essays of the 1930s Horkheimer developed his conception of the role of philosophy primarily through a criticism of modern positivism or empiricism (the terms are used interchangeably), and in particular that of the Vienna Circle. His argument in one important essay, 'The latest attack on metaphysics' (1937), proceeds on two levels. First, in a framework of ideas derived from the sociology of knowledge, he asserts the connection between a style of thought and the situation of a social group, though unlike Karl Mannheim, for example, he does not attempt to analyse the precise filiations between thought and socio-historical conditions. Thus, he simply claims that 'neo-romantic metaphysics and radical positivism alike have their roots in the present sad state of the middle class' (*Critical Theory: Selected Essays*, New York, Herder & Herder, 1972, p. 140), and again, 'the entire system of modern empiricism belongs to the passing world of liberalism' (*ibid.*, p. 147).

At another level Horkheimer undertakes a criticism of positivism as a theory of knowledge or philosophy of science, especially in relation to the social sciences, on three main points: (i) that it treats active human beings as mere facts and objects within a scheme of mechanical determinism; (ii) that it conceives the world only as immediately given in experience, and makes no distinction between essence and appearance; and (iii) that it establishes an absolute distinction between fact and value, and hence separates knowledge from human interests. Horkheimer contrasts with positivism a 'dialectical theory', in which 'individual facts always appear in a definite connection', and which 'seeks to reflect reality in its totality'. Furthermore, dialectical thought 'integrates the empirical constituents into structures of experience which are important . . . for the historical interests with which dialectical thought is connected. . . . When an active individual of sound common sense perceives the sordid state of the world, desire to change it becomes the guiding principle by which he organizes given facts and shapes them into a theory. . . . Right thinking depends as much on right willing as right willing on right thinking' (*ibid.*, pp. 161–2).[2]

Horkheimer pursued this argument in his best known essay of the 1930s, 'Traditional and critical theory' (1937), which should perhaps be regarded as the founding document, or charter, of the Frankfurt School. 'Traditional theory' is there interpreted as the implicit or explicit outlook of the modern natural sciences, expressed in modern philosophy as positivism/empiricism; and Horkheimer is above all concerned with the diffusion of this conception of theory in the 'sciences of man and society [which] have attempted to follow the lead of the natural sciences' (*ibid.*, p. 190). The opposed kind of social thought, 'critical theory', rejects the procedure of determining objective facts with the aid of conceptual systems, from a purely external standpoint, and claims that 'the facts, as they emerge from the work of society, are not extrinsic in the same degree as they are for the savant . . . critical thinking . . . is motivated today by the effort really to transcend the tension and to abolish the opposition between the individual's purposefulness, spontaneity, and rationality, and those work-process relationships on which society is built' (pp. 209–210). But how, in that case, is critical thought related to experience? Is it anything more than 'conceptual poetry' or an 'impotent expression of states of mind'? Marx and Engels had grounded their critical theory in the situation of the proletariat, which necessarily struggles for emancipation. But Horkeimer argues (like Lukács in *History and Class Consciousness*) that even this situation of the proletariat is 'no guarantee of correct knowledge', for 'even to the proletariat the world superficially seems quite different than it really is' (pp. 213–14). He does not then draw the conclusion which Lukács, actively engaged in political life, drew – namely, that a revolutionary party must bring a correct class consciousness (i.e. correct knowledge) to the working class from outside – but there is nevertheless some similarity in their views, for insofar as any very definite conclusion at all can be derived from Horkheimer's discussion it is that another external agent – the critical thinker, or critical school of thought – has the task of conveying such a consciousness to the working class.

Two aspects of Horkheimer's original formulation of critical theory which will be more closely examined in Chapter 3, should be particularly noted at this stage: first, that his hesitant and somewhat sceptical evaluation of the role of the working class already gave an intimation of his later profound pessimism about the existence of any real emancipatory force in modern society; and second, that the political significance which he attributed to the work of critical intellectuals was a reversion to a pre-Marxian conception of the processes of social change, closely resembling the outlook of the Young Hegelians, or 'critical critics', of the late 1830s and early 1840s, which Marx had derided in *The Holy Family*.[3] Similar features, as we shall see, are to be found in the work of Herbert Marcuse, the other major contributor to the formation of critical theory in its early stages. In several essays of the 1930s, and especially in his book *Reason and Revolution* (1941), Marcuse also expounded a 'dialectical social theory' in opposition to a positivist social science, and made much the same points about the latter as Horkheimer had done, arguing that 'positive philosophy tended to equate the study of society with the study of nature. . . . Social study was to be a science seeking social laws, the validity of which was to be analogous to that of physical laws. Social practice, especially the matter of changing the social system, was herewith throttled by the inexorable' (*op. cit.*, p. 343). Where he differed from Horkheimer was in basing the dialectical theory much more directly upon Hegel's philosophy, which constitutes the core of his whole exposition; in transforming

Marx's thought more completely into a radical Hegelianism; and in confining his attention to the origins of positivist philosophy and social science in the first half of the nineteenth century (in the works of Comte, Stahl, and von Stein), while ignoring the modern forms of positivism and related philosophies of science as well as the modern social sciences.

Adorno's contribution to the formation of a school of critical theory is much more ambiguous and obscure. Until 1938 his relations with the Institute were informal, and his principal interests lay in the field of culture (particularly music), psychoanalysis, and aesthetic theory (where he was profoundly influenced by Walter Benjamin).[4] The philosophical outlook which he developed during this time was not a 'dialetical social theory', but what he later called 'negative dialectics'; that is, a criticism of *all* philosophical positions and social theories. This appears to be a form of relativism or scepticism, which denies the possibility of any absolute starting point ('identity-principle') or ultimate basis for human thought, though Adorno attempted to evade this outcome.[5] At all events his philosophical stance is very different from that of Horkheimer or Marcuse, both of whom tried to formulate a positive social theory on the basis of a Hegelian concept of 'reason'. Adorno was also much more remote from Marxism than his colleagues. In his inaugural lecture at the University of Frankfurt, 'The actuality of philosophy' (1931), he expounded a view of philosophy which claimed to be both 'dialectical' and 'materialist', but as Buck-Morss comments '. . . it was not dialectical materialism in any orthodox sense . . . throughout his life he differed fundamentally from Marx in that his philosophy never included a theory of political action'.[6] Moreover, unlike Horkheimer and Marcuse, who only gradually abandoned their (qualified) belief in the revolutionary potential of the working class, Adorno seems never to have given any serious attention to Marx's economic analysis or his theory of class, and he rejected entirely the idea of a theory of history, or 'science of history', which is one of the fundamental elements in Marx's thought. From his early contact with Lukács's writings Adorno retained only 'the negative level of *Ideologiekritik*, the critique of bourgeois class consciousness',[7] not the programme of political action founded upon a Hegelian–Marxist interpretation of history.

Indeed, cultural criticism was to be Adorno's principal contribution to critical theory, as became apparent initially in the work which he wrote with Horkheimer, published as *Dialectic of Enlightenment* (1944).[8] The principal theme of the book, formulated in the introduction, is the 'self-destruction of the Enlightenment' – that is, of reason conceived as a negative, critical treatment of the facts – through the 'false clarity' achieved in scientific thought and the positivist philosophy of science. This modern, scientific consciousness is held to be the main source of the cultural decline as a result of which humanity 'instead of entering into a truly human condition, is sinking into a new kind of barbarism'. Hence, in the first part of the book the criticism of positivism is pursued, and this is now linked with a criticism of science and technology that foreshadows the later treatment of them as 'ideologies' which make possible and help to constitute new forms of domination. The contrast with scientific thought is provided by art, which 'as an expression of totality . . . lays claim to the dignity of the absolute' (*op. cit.*, p. 19). The second major essay in the book is devoted to a subject which became one of the chief preoccupations of the Frankfurt School, namely the 'culture industry', or 'enlightenment as mass deception'. The argument deployed here is not that of Marx, according to which 'the ruling ideas in every age are the ideas of the ruling class' and modern technology might be regarded as having increased the effectiveness with which these ideas are implanted in society at large (a hypothesis to be tested by empirical studies), but rather that technology and a technological consciousness have themselves produced a new phenomenon in the shape of a uniform and debased 'mass culture' which aborts and silences criticism. Adornos' conception of this mass culture was a striking contrast with the view of Benjamin, whose work had profoundly influenced his aesthetic theory at an earlier stage; for Benjamin considered that 'mechanical reproduction' had revolutionary implications inasmuch as it tended to destroy the elitist 'aura' of art and led to a 'tremendous shattering of tradition'. The root of the disagreement between Adorno and Benjamin which developed in the 1930s was political, as Buck-Morss has shown,[9] for under Brecht's influence Benjamin 'expressed solidarity with the working class (and with the Communist Party) by affirming the concept of a collective revolutionary subject', a concept which Adorno, then and later, rejected entirely.

The overriding concern of the Frankfurt School with cultural phenomena – that is, with the manifestations and products of human consciousness – also involved a particular interest in the individual as a centre of thought and action, and in psychology, especially in the form of psychoanalysis. Horkheimer, according to Jay, derived from his early studies of Kant a 'sensitivity to the importance of individuality, as a value never to be submerged entirely under the demands of the totality', and he 'gave qualified praise to the emphasis upon the individual in the work of both Dilthey and Nietzsche'.[10] More generally, Horkheimer was sympathetic to some aspects of *Lebensphilosophie*, as it was called in Germany, a form of what became widely known later as existentialism, which was taking shape at this time notably in the thought of Jean-Paul Sartre, with an equally strong emphasis on the individual. There is also a marked affinity with the earlier preoccupation of Max Weber with the fate of the individual in modern capitalist society;[11] but it is not apparent that Horkheimer or other members of the school paid any detailed attention to Weber's work before the 1960s, though they were undoubtedly influenced by it.[12]

Horkheimer also argued, in an essay on history and psychology published in the first issue of the Institute's journal, the *Zeitschrift für Sozialforschung*, that individual psychology was of great importance for the understanding of history,[13] and in the same issue another essay, by Erich Fromm,[14] set out to establish a relation between psychoanalysis and Marxism by extending Freud's explanations in terms of the history of the individual to include the class location of the family and the historical situation of social classes. In later works Fromm pursued this aim of constructing a Marxist social psychology into which a revised Freudian theory could be incorporated, notably in his model of the 'social character', formulated in an appendix to *The Fear of Freedom*.[15] By this time, however, Fromm had ceased to have any connection with the Institute, and his increasingly sociological (and at the same time more empirical and more Marxist) reinterpretation of psychoanalysis provoked criticism in due course from both Adorno and Marcuse.[16]

The principal interest of the Frankfurt School remained in the sphere of individual psychology, and with the rise of National Socialism in Germany it became concentrated upon two specific questions: personality traits in relation to authority, and anti-Semitism. In the first area the Institute had already initiated research into workers' attitudes in the early 1930s (with Fromm as the director of the project) but this was never published, and the first published study on the subject of the 'authoritarian character' was a collective work, *Studien über Autorität und Familie* (Paris, Felix Alcan, 1936), the first part consisting of three long theoretical essays by Horkheimer, Fromm, and Marcuse, the second part being a series of fragmentary empirical studies. There were considerable differences between the three essays, that of Marcuse (who had only a slight acquaintance with psychoanalysis at the time) being limited to a histori-cal–philosophical discussion of ideas of freedom and authority; but the general approach of the book was clearly expressed by Hork-heimer in the introduction and in his own essay, where he set out the reasons for concentrating upon the cultural aspects of modern society – that is, on the formation of ideas and attitudes – and in particular on the role of the family, and more recently of other social institutions, in creating an 'authoritarian personality'.

In the next stage of the Institute's work in exile these analyses of authoritarianism merged into a large-scale project of research, mainly into anti-Semitism (the *Studies in Prejudice*) which resulted in the publication of five related studies, the best known being *The Authoritarian Personality*.[17] The latter work had a considerable influence and gave rise to much further research, most of which, however, had little or no connection with critical theory.[18] One notable feature of these studies is the almost exclusive concern with subjective, psychological explanations of prejudice, so that two cri-tics of *The Authoritarian Personality* could object that its authors 'take the irrationality out of the social order and impute it to the respon-dent'.[19] To such criticisms it may be replied that Horkheimer and Adorno provided elsewhere a more sociological account of anti-Semitism, particularly in the essay on 'Elements of anti-Semitism' in *Dialectic of Enlightenment*, where they wrote, for example, that 'bourgeois anti-Semitism has a specific economic reason; the con-cealment of domination in production'; but they did not pursue the subject in any depth, and this essay too is largely concerned with the formation of (morbid, paranoiac) perceptions and attitudes which can be interpreted in psychoanalytic terms.

What is most striking of all, however, in the analysis of fascism (more particularly, National Socialism in Germany) by Horkheimer and Adorno is that they virtually identified it with anti-Semitism, or at least came to view it almost exclusively from this narrow perspec-tive. In this respect their work is in sharp contrast with a classic Marxist study of National Socialism, Franz Neumann's *Behemoth*, which concluded that 'the German economy of today . . . is a mono-polistic economy – *and* a command economy. It is a capitalistic economy, regimented by the totalitarian state. We suggest as a name best to describe it, 'Totalitarian Monopoly Capitalism'.[20] It has sometimes been argued that Neumann represented a second approach, within the Frankfurt School, to the study of fascism; but this is misleading, for Neumann was only briefly a member of the

Institute (from 1936 to 1942) and he was remote in his theoretical orientation – which was much more that of classical
Marxism, emphasizing the preponderant influence of the economy,
the class structure, and class struggles – from the ideas of the emerging school of critical theory. Indeed, in *Behemoth* he criticized
explicitly the analysis of National Socialism made by Pollock (who
belonged to the inner circle of the Frankfurt School), who defined
the regime as one of 'state capitalism' in which the profit motive had
been 'superseded by the power motive',[21] and regarded it as a
'new order' in which technical rationality had become the guiding
principle of society.[22] Thus within a body of thought which was
broadly Marxist, or at least derived from Marxism, two very different conceptions of National Socialism were formulated: that of
Neumann which regarded the totalitarian regime as corresponding
with a particular stage in the economic development of capitalism,
its late monopoly stage; and that of Horkheimer and Pollock which
treated it rather as a new type of society, characterized by the 'primacy of politics' over the economy, and by domination exercised
through 'technological rationality' and through the exploitation of
irrational sentiments and attitudes among the mass of the population (e.g. anti-Semitism).[23]

The *Studies in Prejudice* were empirical investigations, and as we
have seen, Horkheimer, on becoming director of the Institute, had
launched an empirical study of workers' attitudes in Germany. In
exile the question of the relation between critical theory and empirical research emerged in a more acute form, for the development of a
distinctive school of social theory, hostile to positivism/empiricism,
took place in an environment in which the social sciences were
oriented primarily to empirical investigations. To a great extent the
leading members of the Institute remained aloof from the mainstream of American social science, as they were able to do by virtue of
their independent financial endowment. Thus, for example, their
journal, the *Zeitschrift für Sozialforschung* continued to be published
mainly in German until 1939 (when it became *Studies in Philosophy
and Social Science*), and they maintained close links with Europe, and
especially with Germany, so far as the circumstances allowed.
Nonetheless, members of the Institute did eventually become
involved in empirical research in various ways – particularly
through the relationship with Paul Lazarsfeld, and through the
Studies in Prejudice project[24] – and they were obliged to consider
more directly the relation between theory and research in the
framework of a scheme of thought which asserted the primacy of
theory.

It cannot be said that this question was explored in any great detail, or in a systematic way, by members of the school during its formative period. Aside from a brief and not particularly illuminating contrast drawn by Horkheimer between 'the traditional inductive method' and the method proper to critical theory, which 'should seek the universal within the particular',[25] there was, in fact, little attempt to relate the theory of society as expounded in *Dialectic of Enlightenment* to the Institute's empirical research, which seems to have been confined to a separate sphere, and was motivated partly by the preoccupation with anti-Semitism, partly by a financial crisis which made it imperative to obtain a grant if the Institute were to survive.[26] Only much later did Adorno – whose contributions to *The Authoritarian Personality* raised no important theoretical questions – expound more fully his position in relation to empirical research, notably in his reflections on his experiences as a European scholar in America[27] and in his contributions to the 'debate about positivism'.[28] These works, however, belong to the following period, the 'golden age' of the Frankfurt School, and they will be examined in that broader context in the next chapter.

By the end of the 1940s the lineaments of a new social theory, or social philosophy, had been presented in two major texts, *Dialectic of Enlightenment* and Marcuse's *Reason and Revolution*, and in a number of essays, which made clear its central preoccupations. A pre-eminent place was occupied by the criticism and rejection of positivism/empiricism, and more broadly of any conception of a 'science of society', to which was opposed a philosophical idea of 'reason', as capable of discovering the essence of phenomena by contrast with 'appearances' or mere facticity. Reason was also conceived, in a generally Hegelian sense, as being intimately connected with freedom; from this standpoint, therefore, knowledge of the world and the determination of authentic values coincide, or as Horkheimer expressed it 'right thinking' and 'right willing' go together in a relationship of mutual support.

The critique of positivism (or better, 'scientism') then merged into a critical assessment of 'scientific and technological rationality' as a new form of domination, characteristic of the late capitalist, or more broadly, the advanced industrial societies of the twentieth century. This was one side of the Frankfurt School's growing emphasis upon ideology as a (if not *the*) major force sustaining domination, and hence upon the criticism of ideology as a major factor in the process of emancipation. The other side was the analysis and criticism of 'irrational' beliefs and attitudes in modern society, especially in the form of anti-Semitism. The preoccupation with these questions also reinforced the school's interest in the psychology of the individual, and in psychoanalytic theory, as a necessary element in any study of the relation between social conditions and social movements; more particularly in considering either the failure of the working class to become a revolutionary force, or the rise of fascist movements.

During its formative period, and still more in its later phases, the Frankfurt School detached itself increasingly from Marx's theory and from classical Marxism, abandoning large (and crucial) parts of that theory, but without embarking upon a systematic critical confrontation with it. Only at a still later date, above all in the work of Habermas, was Marx's own theory subjected to a rigorous critical scrutiny and reconstruction; but this belongs to a distinct post-Marxist, post-Frankfurt School phase of critical theory which will be the subject of a later chapter.

NOTES

[1]   'Die gegenwärtige Lage der Sozialphilosophie und die Aufgaben eines Instituts fur Sozialforschung'.

[2]   Horkheimer's criticisms of positivism and his formulation of an alternative theory are, of course, themselves open to fundamental criticism, and I shall examine them from this standpoint in the following chapters.

[3]   As George Lichtheim noted in the title essay of *From Marx to Hegel* (London, Orbach and Chambers, 1971).

[4]   See the study by Susan Buck-Morss, *The Origin of Negative Dialectics: Theodor W. Adorno, Walter Benjamin, and the Frankfurt School* (Brighton, Harvester Press, 1977).

[5]   For a powerful criticism of Adorno's philosophical writings, see Leszek Kolakowski, *Main Currents of Marxism* (Oxford, Oxford University Press, 1978), Vol. III, pp. 357–69.

[6]   Susan Buck-Morss, *op. cit.*, p. 24.

[7]   *Ibid.*, p. 26.

[8]   English edn. New York, Herder & Herder, 1972.

[9]   Buck-Morss, *op. cit.*, chaps 9–10. See also the discussion of Benjamin in relation to the Frankfurt School in Dave Laing, *The Marxist Theory of Art* (Brighton, Harvester Press, 1978), especially chap. 6.

[10] Martin Jay, *The Dialectical Imagination* (Boston, Little, Brown & Co., 1973), pp. 46, 49.

[11]   See Karl Löwith, *Max Weber and Karl Marx* (London, Allen & Unwin, 1982).

[12]   The principal critical discussion of Weber, from quite another aspect, is that by Marcuse, in his essay of 1964 on 'Industrialisation and Capitalism', in Otto Stammer (ed.), *Max Weber and Sociology Today* (Oxford, Blackwell, 1971). See also pp. 36–7 below.

[13]   Horkheimer, 'Geschichte und Psychologie', *Zeitschrift für Sozialforschung*, **I**, 1/2 (1932).

[14]   'The Method and Function of an Analytic Social Psychology: Notes on Psychoanalysis and Historical Materialism', in Erich Fromm, *The Crisis of Psychoanalysis* (New York, Holt, Rinehart & Winston, 1970).

[15]   Erich Fromm, *The Fear of Freedom* (London, Routledge & Kegan Paul, 1942), pp. 239–53.

[16]   Adorno, 'Social Science and Sociological Tendencies in Psychoanalysis' (1946, unpublished paper; German version in *Sociologica II; Reden und Vorträge*, ed. Max Horkheimer and Theodor W. Adorno (Frankfurt, Europäische Verlagsanstalt, 1962)); Marcuse, *Eros and Civilization: A Philosophical Inquiry into Freud* (Boston, Beacon Press, 1955).

[17]   T. W. Adorno, Else Frenkel-Brunswik, Daniel J. Levinson, and R. Nevitt Sandford, *The Authoritarian Personality* (New York, Harper & Row, 1950).

[18]   For an account of some of this research, as well as critical comments on the original study, see Richard Christie and Marie Jahoda (eds), *Studies in the Scope and Method of 'The Authoritarian Personality'* (Glencoe, Free Press, 1954).

[19]   Herbert H. Hyman and Paul B. Sheatsley, *'The Authoritarian Personality* – a Methodological Critique', in Christie and Jahoda, *op. cit.*

[20]   Franz Neumann, *Behemoth: The Structure and Practice of National Socialism* (New York, Oxford University Press, 1942, new edn, 1944) p. 261.

[21]   Friedrich Pollock, 'State Capitalism: Its Possibilities and Limitations', *Studies in Philosophy and Social Science*, **IX**, 2 (1941).

[22]   *Idem*, 'Is National Socialism a New Order?', *Studies in Philosophy and Social Science*, **IX**, 3 (1941).

[23]   There were also, of course, other Marxist analyses of Fascism which drew attention to additional elements involved in its rise; for example, Otto Bauer, 'Fascism' (1938; English trans-

lation in Bottomore and Goode, *Austro-Marxism* (Oxford, Oxford University Press, 1978)), and Leon Trotsky, *The Struggle Against Fascism in Germany* (Articles of 1930–33; New York, Pathfinder, 1971).

[24] For a fuller account see Jay, *op. cit.*, pp. 189–93 and chap. VII.

[25] Horkheimer, 'Notes on Institute Activities', *Studies in Philosophy and Social Science* **IX**, 1 (1941).

[26] See Jay, *op. cit.*, pp. 220–1.

[27] Adorno, 'Scientific Experiences of a European Scholar in America', in *The Intellectual Migration: Europe and America, 1930–1960*, Donald Fleming and Bernard Bailyn (eds), (Cambridge, Mass., Harvard University Press, 1969).

[28] Adorno *et al.*, *The Positivist Dispute in German Sociology* 1969. (English translation, London, Heinemann, 1976.)

2

The High Tide of Critical Theory

After its return to Frankfurt in 1950 the Institute was entirely dominated by the ideas of Horkheimer and Adorno; more particularly the latter, since Horkheimer was frequently absent between 1954 and 1959 as a visiting professor at the University of Chicago, and retired in 1959. In its revived form the Institute assumed the character of a well-defined school of thought, pre-eminently a school of philosophy and of aesthetic theory, these being Adorno's own primary interests. Its distinctive orientation is evident also in the work of the second generation of scholars associated with it, the most prominent of whom – Jürgen Habermas, Alfred Schmidt, Albrecht Wellmer – were all philosophers. Among the older members of the Institute who remained in the USA Marcuse at least can likewise be considered as a leading figure in the new school, although differences between its European and American adherents emerged later, especially with regard to political action.

The philosophical character of the School became steadily more pronounced through the 1950s and 1960s, notwithstanding the fact that Adorno, on first returning to Germany, had advocated the use of empirical methods (though not in order to test theories) and had argued that sociology should no longer be regarded as a *Geisteswis-*

senschaft (a cultural science) to be pursued by the interpretation of 'meaning'. [1] By the time of his paper at the Fourth World Congress of Sociology in 1959 Adorno had resumed his criticism of what he called a 'non-philosophical' (and in this specific sense 'non-theoretical') sociology, which 'in terms of its mere structure of categories, elevates the simple reproduction of what exists to an ideal. . . . Positivism is an attitude which not only clings to what is given, but takes a positive view of it'; [2] and the attack upon positivism became the *leitmotiv* of his work for the next decade.

The criticism of positivism and empiricism, and the attempt to formulate an alternative epistemology and methodology for social theory, provided not only the foundation, but also a large part of the substance of the Frankfurt School's theory of society over three decades, from Horkheimer's essay on traditional and critical theory in 1937 to the debate about positivism in 1969, and it is this central core of their doctrine which must now be more closely examined. In broad outline, their criticism had three distinct aspects, which I shall consider in turn: first, that positivism is an inadequate and misleading approach which does not, and cannot, attain a true conception or understanding of social life; second, that by attending only to what exists it sanctions the present social order, obstructs any radical change, and leads to political quietism; third, that it is intimately connected with, and is indeed a major factor in sustaining, or producing, a new form of domination, namely 'technocratic domination'.

In criticizing positivism as a theory of knowledge and philosophy of science the Frankfurt School thinkers operated with a rather imprecise and variable notion of the object of their criticism. [3] Thus Marcuse, in *Reason and Revolution*, concentrated his attention on the positivism of Comte (and its German counterpart in the works of F. J. Stahl and Lorenz von Stein), as 'a conscious reaction against the critical and destructive tendencies of French and German rationalism';[4] in short, as a counter-revolutionary doctrine. Horkheimer, in his two major essays published in 1937 [5] criticized positivism more comprehensively as a philosophy of science, especially in the form of the 'logical positivism' or 'logical empiricism' of the Vienna Circle. His criticism was directed broadly against all versions of 'scientism' (i.e. against the idea of a universal scientific method, common to the natural and the social sciences, which was expressed by members of the Vienna Circle in the project of a 'unified science'), [6] and in particular against its claim that science is '*the* knowledge and *the* theory' and its disparagement of philosophy

'. . . that is, every critical attitude towards science'. He continued by saying that 'it is true that any position which is manifestly irreconcilable with definite scientific views must be considered false . . . [but] constructive thought brings together conceptions of various disciplines [and] weaves them into the right pattern for the given situation. This positive connection with science does not mean that the language of science is the true and proper form of knowledge . . . it is naive and bigoted to think and speak only in the language of science'. [7] Horkheimer's contrast between traditional and critical theory begins from the conception of science as a social activity. The traditional idea of theory corresponds to the scientific activity of the savant within the division of labour 'which takes place alongside all the other activities of a society, but in no immediately clear connection with them [and] the real social function of science is not made manifest'; this 'false consciousness of the bourgeois savant in the liberal era' is expressed in diverse philosophies of science, especially in the Neo-Kantianism of the Marburg school. [8] Thinkers who adopt the 'critical attitude', on the other hand, recognize 'the two-sided character of the social totality in its present form', the antagonisms, particularly class conflicts, within it, and while they 'identify themselves with this totality and conceive it as will and reason' they also 'experience the fact that society is comparable to non-human natural processes, to pure mechanisms, because cultural forms which are supported by war and oppression are not the creations of a unified, self-conscious will'. [9] Hence, 'critical acceptance of the categories which rule social life contains simultaneously their condemnation', [10] and the aim of critical theory becomes manifest as the transformation of society and human emancipation. This attempt to synthesize knowledge and purpose, theoretical and practical reason, became and remained a fundamental philosophical position of the Frankfurt School, and the ground of its criticism of the positivist separation of 'fact' and 'value'.

Horkheimer then went on to consider the relation between traditional and critical theory from another aspect: 'If a theoretical procedure [critical theory] does not take the form of determining objective facts with the help of the simplest and most differentiated conceptual systems available, what can it be but an aimless intellectual game, half conceptual poetry, half impotent expression of states of mind?' [11] His way of resolving this problem, identical with that of Lukács (and the profound influence of Lukács's *History and Class Consciousness* is evident throughout this section of the essay), is to argue that the emancipatory concern of critical theory has its basis in the situation of the proletariat in modern society; and the qualification he introduces, that even the situation of the proletariat is no guarantee of correct knowledge, also does not diverge from the view of Lukács, who distinguished between the 'empirical class consciousness' of the proletariat (which might well be false) and a 'correct class consciousness' (which had to be brought to it from outside). Horkheimer expressed this idea by saying that the real social function of the critical theorist emerges when he and his work 'are seen as forming a dynamic unity with the oppressed class, so that his presentation of societal contradictions is not merely an expression of the concrete historical situation but also a force within it to stimulate change'.[12] The fundamental difference between Lukács and Horkheimer was that while the former specified a precise social location for this dynamic unity in the revolutionary party (admittedly an 'ideal' party which was in stark contrast with the actual Bolshevik party of which he was a member), the latter gave no indication at all of where the interaction between thinker and class would take place (surely not in the University and its research institutes?). And by the 1950s when Horkheimer (like other Frankfurt School thinkers) had lost completely his vestigial belief in the revolutionary potential of the working class, critical theory appeared to lack any ground whatsoever in actual social life, and he was led eventually, as we shall see, to adopt a religious justification of it.

In these early essays Horkheimer also formulated a number of specific criticisms of logical positivism [13] which became generally held tenets of the Frankfurt School: namely, that verification through perception, 'the alpha and omega of empiricism', is an inadequate principle, which indicates the 'increasing shallowness of bourgeois thought'; that positivism involves an accumulation of 'solitary facts', more or less arbitrarily 'selected from the infinite number that present themselves'; and that positivism makes no distinction between the surface appearance of things and their core or 'essence'. 'The facts of science and science itself', he concluded, 'are but segments of the life process of society, and in order to understand the significance of facts or of science generally one must possess the key to the historical situation, the right social theory'. [14] Furthermore, this 'right social theory' depends crucially, as I noted earlier (p. 16 above), upon 'right willing'. Some of the criticisms of modern positivism sketched by Horkheimer were of course also taken up in a more thorough and systematic way in other philosophies of science, that of Popper, for example, and more recently by structuralists and realists, but the Frankfurt School contribution to these later debates was slight until the work of Habermas (which will be discussed in the next chapter).

Adorno, in his essays of the 1950s and 1960s, [15] largely repeated the criticisms of positivism already formulated by Horkheimer, and in particular those directed against its preoccupation with 'facts' (i.e. superficial phenomena) and its alleged 'positive' evaluation of the existing state of society. However, in one late text, his introduction to the 'debate about positivism',[16] which was originally supposed to be a debate between him and Popper,[17] Adorno introduced some new elements into critical theory. In response to Popper's well-founded objection that he had never been a 'positivist', but a critic of the positivism of the Vienna Circle from a realist standpoint, Adorno proposed to refer to his conception as 'scientistic', but he did not go on to examine the various forms of, or arguments for, 'scientism', and indeed he paid little further attention to Popper's theses about the tasks of the theoretical social sciences. Instead, he embarked upon a discussion of ontology and epistemology, rather than the philosophy of science or methodology, from the standpoint of his conception of 'negative dialectics'. [18] A discussion of Adorno's philosophical views lies outside the scope of the present book, [19] and I shall consider them here only in their bearing upon the idea of a critical theory of society. From this point of view Adorno's thought introduces several very important modifications of the Frankfurt School theory as Horkheimer had expounded it. In the first place, critical theory is now represented as being purely critical, incapable of formulating any positive conceptions at all (for example, a positive alternative to the existing society) since any such formulation would involve 'identity-thinking' (i.e. the assertion of an absolute starting-point for philosophy, and more particularly with regard to epistemology, a conception of the world as a constellation of empirical objects which can be adequately grasped by means of appropriate concepts). Second, the notion of 'totality', which was crucial in Horkheimer's thought (one of his criticisms of positivism being that it did not situate individual facts within a totality as did critical theory), is now rejected as another manifestation of identity-thinking; in Adorno's phrase, 'the whole is untrue'. Whether Adorno's philosophy is free from self-contradiction is not an issue to be pursued here. [20] What is clear, at all events, is that it tends towards scepticism, and is quite incompatible, not only with Marxism (for Marx undeniably formulated a positive theory of history and a theory of capitalist society, which he believed to be well grounded), but with any kind of systematic social theory. Adorno's late philosophy signals the beginning of the decline of the Frankfurt School.

The second theme in the Frankfurt School criticism of positivism is that of the connection between a positivist philosophy of science (or more broadly a positivist 'world view') and an acceptance of the *status quo*. It is difficult to interpret the argument on this point, and indeed the claim that there *is* a connection is asserted rather than argued, from the early expositions of critical theory up to the period of its maturity. Should we, for example, take the relation to be a logical one, in the sense that a positivistically conceived social science necessarily entails a specific (in some way conservative) view of politics? This question was never clearly posed or analysed by the Frankfurt School, but it is not difficult to see the weaknesses in a claim such as that of Marcuse, that 'a science seeking social laws' would inexorably throttle 'social practice, especially the matter of changing the social system'. [21] For Marx not only sought, but formulated, social laws which specified the structural contradictions and social antagonisms in capitalist society (and in preceding forms of society), and the inherent tendencies to change. From this aspect it may be said that the link between critical theory and Marxism became increasingly tenuous, and a later work explicitly rejected the 'latent positivism' of Marx's theory; [22] but it can scarcely be claimed that Marx's 'positivism' was associated with a conservative view of politics (though of course he may have misunderstood the logic of his own theory and held beliefs which were in fact incompatible).

In the later development of the Frankfurt School's conception of the relation between positivism and politics what came to be most strongly emphasized was the idea of a 'scientific politics' (excluding value judgements or any consideration of inequalities of power) which was allegedly entailed by a positivist philosophy of science. This 'scientization' of politics is examined in several essays by Habermas in the late 1960s, [23] but it is there treated more as the direct consequence of the economic and social importance of science and technology, rather than of a theory of science, and I shall consider it from this point of view below. The most systematic analysis of the conceptual link between positivism and scientific politics (or a 'social engineering' conception of political practice) is to be found, not in the principal works of the Frankfurt School in this period, but in a later study by Brian Fay, [24] who, while sympathetic to critical theory, also attempts to construct a different model of a critical social science which incorporates some elements of positivism (e.g.

its intention to discover quasi-causal laws). Fay's argument, very briefly summarized, is that 'the possibility of technical control, far from having a contingent relationship to science, is indeed part of the framework which constitutes the very possibility of scientific activity', and hence 'a positivist conception of the knowledge of social life contains within itself an instrumentalist-engineering conception of the relation of this knowledge to social action'.[25] This kind of argument is in turn criticized by Russell Keat, who propounds the view that 'neither scientism nor the positivist view of science entail the possibility of a scientific politics, since both are consistent with the claim that political decisions cannot be made solely by reference to scientific knowledge'. [26]

These controversies, however, belong to the post-Frankfurt School era, in which new philosophies of science and much more subtle and discriminating conceptions of positivism were elaborated, and they will be more closely considered, also in relation to the work of Habermas, in a later chapter. In the present context, what should be noted further is that whereas the idea of 'scientific politics' (as an outcome of positivism) was equated by the Frankfurt School thinkers with conservative politics, or the defence of the *status quo*, the same idea, oddly enough, could be presented by a conservative theorist, F. A. Hayek, as a form of *socialist* politics. Hayek's essays of 1941–44, [27] which were largely responsible for diffusing the terms 'scientism' and 'scientistic' in the English speaking world, [28] set out a criticism of the objectivism, collectivism and historicism of the scientific approach, and went on to consider the practical attitudes which 'spring from' these theoretical views; in particular the demand for conscious control of social processes ('social engineering' and 'socialist planning') which he considered incompatible with the maintenance of a 'free society', the basis of which could only be the individualism of a capitalist economy. It is beyond the scope of this book to consider whether Hayek succeeds any better than the Frankfurt School in establishing a logical connection between a philosophy of science and a particular political practice. What is evident is, on one side, the diversity of possible interpretations of what scientism is and implies, and on the other, certain common elements in their thought, notably the idea that a new type of domination is emerging in modern societies which is in some way connected with the pre-eminence of science and technology.

We have next to consider, therefore, whether the Frankfurt School, if it did not succeed in demonstrating a strict conceptual link between scientism and a political practice which reproduces the existing society, was able to show that there is a psychological and/or sociological connection. This would involve demonstrating, in psychological terms, that those who adopt a scientistic view are also disposed to be politically conservative or acquiescent, and vice versa; but little attempt was made to establish the existence of such a relationship, and the hypothesis seems indeed implausible. In sociological terms, it would be necessary to show that the social location of different intellectual groups inclined them to be scientistic/conservative or the reverse, but again little analysis of this kind was attempted, and it was in fact the Frankfurt School itself which was subsequently examined from this point of view. Jay compares its leading members with the German 'mandarins', the educated elite studied by Ringer, [29] and observes that 'Like the mandarins and unlike more orthodox socialists, they wrote works permeated more with a sense of loss and decline than with expectation and hope. They also shared the mandarins' distaste for mass society and the utilitarian, positivistic values it fostered.' [30] In this respect their attitudes resembled those of Tönnies and Max Weber towards industrial capitalism.

It may also be said of the school's association of scientism with political conservatism or acquiescence that their own anti-scientism did not for the most part save them from a passivity which acquired increasingly conservative overtones. Lukács described their situation by saying that 'many of the leading German intellectuals, including Adorno, have installed themselves in this "Grand Hotel Abyss" which I have described elsewhere in connection with Schopenhauer: "It is a hotel provided with every modern comfort, but resting on the edge of the abyss, of nothingness, of the absurd. The daily contemplation of the abyss, in between the excellent meals and artistic entertainments, can only enhance the residents' enjoyment of this superlative comfort" ' [31] Lukács's judgement may be excessively harsh, but it is undeniably the case that, with the exception of Marcuse, no leading member of the Frankfurt School took any active part in, or gave support to, a radical political movement, and that both Adorno and Horkheimer quickly dissociated themselves from the student movement of the late 1960s, which some of their own writings may be thought to have encouraged. The Frankfurt School thus came to resemble, as Jay also remarks, [32] Mannheim's 'free-floating intellectuals', poised above the *mêlée*.

A sociological account of scientism was first briefly sketched in Horkheimer's essays of the 1930s, where it is treated as a form of bourgeois thought which corresponds in some way with 'modern methods of production'. In this account critical theory was still closely attached, in principle, to Marx's analysis of the economy and the class structure as constituting the real basis of social life,[33] and at the same time paid attention to more recent phenomena – the growth of monopoly, the rise of industrial magnates and managers – which had been extensively studied by other Marxists. Gradually, however, the emphasis changed. In *Dialectics of Enlightenment* it is not so much scientism as a philosophy of science, and an element of bourgeois thought, but science and technology themselves, and the 'technological consciousness' or 'instrumental reason' which they diffuse throughout society (or which somehow accompanies their development) that are now seen as the principal factor in the maintenance of domination. At the same time, domination ceases to be regarded as domination by a particular class, for the class structure of capitalist society, and the conflict between classes, as Marx depicted them, are no longer conceived as important features of the modern Western societies. As Marcuse expressed it in *One Dimensional Man*: 'In the capitalist world, they [bourgeoisie and proletariat] are still the basic classes. However, the capitalist development has altered the structure and function of these two classes in such a way that they no longer appear to be agents of historical transformation. An overriding interest in the preservation and improvement of the institutional status quo unites the former antagonists in the most advanced areas of contemporary society.' Adorno's thought on the subject is more fragmentary and ambiguous. In an earlier essay on the theory of class, written during the National Socialist period, he had argued that the 'oppressed can no longer experience themselves as a class', that instead of the nature of class society becoming absolutely clear it has been mystified by the mass society in which it has culminated, and that the proletariat, contrary to Marx's theory, has become 'socially impotent'.[34] From this standpoint, evidently, class conflict cannot be the driving force of history (at any rate of recent history), which must be sought rather in whatever it is that has brought into existence the 'mass society'. But in an essay of the 1960s Adorno insists that the present-day Western societies (and also those of Eastern Europe) are still class societies, and that the antagonisms within them could at any time destroy organized society in a total catastrophe.[35] Yet later in the same essay he seems to deny this possibility by claiming that in these rationalized societies, and under the influence of the 'culture industry', human beings 'have come to identify themselves (triumph of integration!), even in their innermost patterns of behaviour, with what happens to them'. Again, in his opening address to the German Sociological Conference of 1968, on the theme of whether modern societies should be characterized as 'late capitalism' or 'industrial society',[36] Adorno, after observing that, while classes still exist, there is no working class consciousness, went on to question some of Marx's basic conceptions – surplus value, pauperization, the influence of productive forces on the relations of production – and then pursued an argument which led to the conclusion that 'the system' has become independent of all the members of society, including those in the commanding positions, driven on by the impersonal forces of technological rationality.

This view of the power of technological rationality is stated most fully and systematically, however, in Marcuse's *One-Dimensional Man*, especially in Chapter 6 on the 'logic of domination'. The underlying conception, which became a distinctive tenet of the Frankfurt School in its heyday, is that the domination of nature through science and technology necessarily gives rise to a new form of domination of human beings: 'Society reproduced itself in a growing technical ensemble of things and relations which included the technical utilization of men – in other words, the struggle for existence and the exploitation of man and nature became ever more scientific and rational' (p.146). Marcuse goes on to argue that 'the science of nature develops under the *technological a priori* which projects nature as potential instrumentality [and] . . . the technological *a priori* is a political *a priori* inasmuch as the transformation of nature involves that of man, and inasmuch as the "man-made creations" issue from and re-enter a societal ensemble' (pp. 153–4); and finally, that 'technological rationality thus protects rather than cancels the legitimacy of domination' (pp. 158–9).[37]

There is an unmistakable affinity between this idea of the dominance of technological rationality and Max Weber's notion of the process of 'rationalization' of the modern world; and it has often been remarked that the Frankfurt School thinkers were increasingly influenced by Weber's thought (although, with the exception of Marcuse's essay of 1964,[38] they made only brief references to it), to such an extent indeed that some have interpreted the development of Frankfurt School theory in the 1950s and 1960s as a passage from a Marxian to a Weberian conception of the historical tendencies inherent in advanced industrial societies. The similarities between the Frankfurt School and Weberian interpretations have two principal aspects. First, technological rationality or rationalization are depicted as abstract forces shaping society which are beyond human control; in some way the inner logic of the system created by science and rational administration works itself out behind the backs of individuals or particular social groups, and it does so whatever the apparent form of the society (whether it is, for example, 'capitalist' or 'socialist', 'totalitarian' or 'democratic').[39] In this sense, the concept of 'industrial society' is substituted for that of 'capitalist society', and it depends, as MacIntyre noted, upon 'a fairly crude technological determinism'.[40] Thus Marcuse, in his essay on Weber, argues that 'not only the application of technology but technology itself is domination (of nature and men) – methodical, scientific, calculated, calculating control. Specific purposes and interests of domination are not foisted upon technology "subsequently" and from the outside; they enter the very construction of the technical apparatus.'[41] True, Marcuse continues by saying that 'technology is always a historical–social *project*; in it is projected what a society and its ruling interests intend to do with men and things';[42] but the notion of 'ruling interests' is left unanalysed and vague, and there is no indication whether these are the interests of the bourgeoisie (that is, of capital) or of some other identifiable social group.

The second major similarity between Weber and the Frankfurt School is to be found in the bleak pessimism that emerges from their interpretations of modern industrial society. If Weber was, in Mommsen's words, 'a liberal in despair'[43] then the thinkers of the Frankfurt School, or at any rate Marcuse, can perhaps be described as 'radicals in despair'. For Weber the more or less inexorable extension of rationalization and intellectualization meant that society would come to be dominated by purely instrumental social relationships; it would be an 'iron cage', a state of 'mechanized petrifaction', stifling individual creativity and personal values. Against this threat Weber saw no real and effective defence, only a despairing attempt to maintain some individual values in the purely private sphere, and just possibly the emergence of a charismatic leader who would prove capable of accomplishing a 'transvaluation of all values' (in Nietzsche's sense) and setting social life upon a new course. Marcuse's pessimism (and especially that of Horkheimer in relation to the fate of the individual, which will be discussed later) is of much the same kind. It is technological rationalization (i.e. instrumental reason) which dominates social life, and there are few if any forces to oppose it; Marcuse concludes *One-Dimensional Man* by saying that 'the critical theory of society was, at the time of its origin, confronted with the presence of real forces . . . *in* the established society which moved (or could be guided to move) toward more rational and freer institutions . . . These were the empirical grounds on which the theory was erected . . . Without the demonstration of such forces . . . "liberation of inherent possibilities" no longer adequately expresses the historical alternative' (pp. 254–5). If indeed there is an alternative. Unlike Weber, Marcuse does not see as even a remote possibility of opposition to the 'administered society' the preservation by individuals of a private sphere of values (though Horkheimer was more inclined to this view); the only chance of a revolutionary opposition, and it is a very slight chance, is to be found in the substratum of society, among 'the outcasts and outsiders, the exploited and persecuted of other races and other colours, the unemployed and the unemployable'. Later on in the 1960s, however, with the rise of new radical movements, Marcuse became somewhat more optimistic; for the revolutionary forces now seemed larger, including students, exploited ethnic minorities, and the peasant masses of the Third World.

The despairing outlook of the Frankfurt School in its last phase derives, in a formal sense, from an analysis of modern Western society, but it should also be seen against the wider background of a current of social thought (especially prominent in Germany) which, from the end of the nineteenth century, expressed not only opposition to positivism as a theory of science, but a general hostility to science and technology as such, in terms of their social and cultural consequences. Thus Hughes, in his study of European thought between 1890 and 1930,[44] observes that the revolt against positivism was associated with a questioning of the cult of material progress, and a protest against the 'mechanization of life', which found one kind of expression in neo-romanticism, the *Lebensphilosophie*, and the reassertion of 'spiritual' values, another in Max Weber's gloomy reflections on the rationalization and 'disenchantment' of the world. Subsequently, the convulsions and destruction caused by the First World War, the experience of the National Socialist regime in Germany, the domination and division of the world since 1945 by superpowers increasingly involved in a nuclear arms race, all contributed cumulatively to the sense of cultural loss and decline, and of mounting irrationality.

The Frankfurt School was deeply embedded in this tradition of thought, and its growing influence in the 1960s was undoubtedly connected with the renewal, in a variety of forms, and particularly in some sections of the middle class, of the revulsion against technological and bureaucratic rationalization. At the same time, its criticism of modern society was purportedly founded upon an analysis of the nature of this society, most fully and explicitly presented in Marcuse's *One-Dimensional Man*. What this analysis claims to show is that the two main classes in capitalist society – bourgeoisie and proletariat – have disappeared as effective historical agents; hence there is, on one side, no dominant *class*, but instead domination by an impersonal power ('scientific–technological rationality') and on the other side, no opposing *class*, for the working class has been assimilated and pacified, not only through high mass consumption but in the rationalized process of production itself. Marcuse, however, does not base his analysis upon an empirical study, or upon a careful assessment of the available evidence; he refers vaguely to a 'vast sociological and psychological literature', but concludes that 'perhaps the most telling evidence can be obtained simply by looking at television or listening to the AM radio for one consecutive hour for a couple of days, not shutting off the commercials, and now and then switching the station' (p. xvii). The book consists of philosophical reflections upon advanced industrial society in the USA, repeating the arguments of *Reason and Revolution* in a more popular form, and perhaps achieving no more than what Horkheimer referred to as an 'impotent expression of states of mind'. In particular, it may be noted how far the broad generalizations depend upon an interpretation of a peculiarly American experience of culturally debased commercial radio and television, and of the absence of a politically organized working class since before the First World War.[45]

Nevertheless, Marcuse's ideas evoked a brief response in the American student movement of the late 1960s, with its opposition to 'the system'; and to some extent in the student movements of various European countries. But the social movements of that time were all influenced by much wider-ranging and more diverse analyses of the changing class structure and of the significance of technocracy and bureaucracy, to which sociologists made a notable contribution. Following Weber's account of the inexorable spread of rationalized production and administration there first emerged a theory of the 'managerial revolution'[46] and the early discussions of technocracy,[47] and then more comprehensive studies of 'industrial society' and 'post-industrial society'. The conservative interpretation of these phenomena, for example in the writings of Raymond Aron and Daniel Bell,[48] emphasized above all the gradual obliteration of major class differences (which could also be regarded as the emergence of predominantly 'middle class' societies), the moderation or virtual elimination of class conflict, and the associated decline of 'ideologies' as Aron defined them: 'total systems of interpretation of the historic–political world' (the principal example of such an ideology being, of course, Marxism). The radical interpretation, notably in the writings of Alain Touraine,[49] while claiming that the class structure of nineteenth-century capitalism has been profoundly transformed, argues that a new fundamental rift has appeared in the Western societies (and with due regard to the different context, also in the socialist societies of Eastern Europe),[50] and that new kinds of conflict (exemplified by the actions of social movements, and the reaction against them, since the late 1960s) have partly replaced, partly subsumed, the old style class conflicts. In Touraine's view the major groups engaged in conflict in post-industrial societies (which can also be called 'technocratic' or 'programmed' societies) are no longer the bourgeoisie and the working class, but on one side those who command the structures of economic and political decision-making, and on the other, those who have been reduced to a condition of dependent participation (though the former group of course includes the large owners of capital and the latter includes the industrial workers).

The work of Marxist sociologists diverges significantly from both conservative and radical interpretations of 'post-industrial society', as well as from Marcuse's analysis (which is close to the conservative view in many respects) by its emphasis upon the continuing dominance of capital (more particularly in the form of large corporations and multinationals) and upon the major importance of the traditional labour movement as an agency of social transformation. These sociologists do, of course, take account of the substantial changes in capitalist society during the twentieth century; on one side through the centralization and concentration of capital and the growth of state intervention in the economy, and on the other side, through the (partly related) changes in the class structure, involving particularly the social situation and consciousness of the working class and the growth of the middle class. There are many differences of view among Marxists about the interpretation of these processes of change within capitalism,[51] but at the same time much common ground in the recognition of the crucial and continuing importance of the relation between capital and labour, and its political expression in diverse forms of class struggle, conflict between parties, and the actions of social movements. By contrast with these numerous investigations of 'industrial society' or 'late capitalism' by Marxist and non-Marxist sociologists, it is the absence of any serious and detailed analysis of the capitalist economy, of the class structure, and of the development of political parties and movements which makes the Frankfurt School studies of modern society now seem extraordinarily narrow and inadequate.

We have next to consider a second major theme in the thought of the Frankfurt School – the preoccupation with the fate of the individual in present-day society – which was itself closely related to the idea of domination by 'scientific–technological rationality' and also had an evident affinity with the concerns of Max Weber in his later writings. As I noted earlier (p. 19 above) Horkheimer was from the outset committed to the value of individuality, and he reasserted this commitment, though in a more pessimistic vein,[52] reminiscent of Weber, in essays and interviews of the last decade of his life. Faced with what he saw as 'the trend to a rationalized, automated, totally manged world', in an age which 'tends to eliminate every vestige of even a relative autonomy for the individual',[53] Horkheimer could now see no way of opposing this trend, and protecting, or where possible extending, 'the limited and ephemeral freedom of the individual' except by the assertion of a religious 'yearning for the wholly other'.[54] By the end of his life indeed Horkheimer had ceased to be a 'critical theorist' and had moved to some kind of religious thought. He set Kant and Hegel above Marx, and in the words of Gumnior and Ringguth 'saw the greatness of the German idealists in their affinity with Jewish religiosity and Jewish thought'.[55] Horkheimer himself formulated his later views on religious thought by saying that what is important in theology is 'the consciousness that the world is "appearance", that it is not the absolute truth or ultimate end',[56] and that 'I do not believe there is any philosophy that I could accept which does not include a theological element'.[57]

Adorno and Marcuse had an equally despairing view of the situation of the individual in modern society, but they responded to it in rather different ways. Marcuse, as we have seen, retained a vestigial hope that new revolutionary forces would emerge inside this society, and in his philosophical reinterpretation of Freud[58] he argued that with the overcoming of material scarcity in the advanced industrial societies the conditions had been established for human beings to attain the goal of happiness through sexual liberation and the supremacy of the 'pleasure principle', conceived as the basis of a comprehensive emancipation affecting all social relations. Adorno, however, saw the possibility of liberating the individual from domination neither in the rise of new oppositional groups, nor in sexual liberation, but rather in the work of the 'authentic' artist, who confronts the given reality with intimations of what it could be.

Authentic art has therefore a subversive potential, and Adorno contrasts it, as a superior form of cognition – a future-oriented pursuit of truth – with science, which only reflects the existing reality.[59]

From a sociological perspective two questions have to be posed about the Frankfurt School thinkers' view of the condition of the individual in advanced industrial society. The first is whether their account is descriptively true. Here we encounter a familiar difficulty, for there is no attempt to establish empirically that significant changes have occurred; at most there is the assertion of a contrast with the supposedly autonomous bourgeois individual of liberal capitalist society. It is doubtful whether this sweeping distinction itself can be upheld, at any rate in more than a tentative way, without numerous qualifications (not least in respect of the differences between nations and national traditions), and any attempt to establish it more convincingly would require the kind of thorough historical research which the Frankfurt School consistently eschewed. More important still is the fact that the entire discussion centres upon the *bourgeois* individual. The Frankfurt School thinkers paid no attention to the growth of freedom and autonomy after 1945 for a large proportion of the population in the industrial countries, which resulted from changes in the balance of social power, modest no doubt, but real, between labour and capital, with the extension of welfare services and education, full employment, and the greater strength of trade unions. The mundane, but very important freedoms, including a considerable expansion of leisure time, gained in this period have to be set against the tendencies to more intensive regulation and control through the processes of rationalized production and administration. Even in the socialist societies of Eastern Europe there are similar gains to be counted against obvious losses, though the conception of a 'totally administered society' may seem more relevant there, except that the power which dominates those societies is not 'scientific–technological rationality' but a political party or perhaps a new ruling class. In the capitalist societies the economic crisis of the 1980s has produced a counter-offensive of capital against labour, which manifestly undermines the freedom and autonomy of those in the subordinate class by depriving them of employment, eroding the social services, and generally subjecting individuals to harsher kinds of economic compulsion. Reading the Frankfurt School texts on the loss of individual autonomy (and especially the writings of Adorno and Horkheimer) it is difficult to escape the impression that what they express above all, as did the similar texts of Max Weber, is the sense of decline in a particular stratum of society, that of the educated upper middle class, or more specifically the 'mandarins', and the nostalgia for a traditional German *Kultur*.

The second question to be considered is whether the Frankfurt School's preoccupation with the fate of the individual led, in another direction, through the interest in psychology and psychoanalysis which it helped to inspire, to any theoretical reformulation of the relation between individual and society. In the early years of the school, as we have seen, Erich Fromm set out to relate Freud's psychology of the individual to Marx's social theory by emphasizing particularly the location of the family in a historically created class structure, while rejecting Freud's transhistorical theory of culture. Subsequently, after he had severed his connection with the Frankfurt School, Fromm pursued his exploration of the relation between psychoanalysis and Marxism in various directions, by formulating the idea of the 'social character' (in *The Fear of Freedom*), by revising radically Freud's conception of human nature and human needs, and by taking as the central theme of Marx's social thought, most fully expressed in the *Economic and Philosophical Manuscripts*, the overcoming of 'alienation'.[60]

It is more difficult to follow the development of Frankfurt School thought on this subject. In the studies undertaken during the period of exile in the USA, and notably in *The Authoritarian Personality*, the psychology of the individual was most strongly emphasized, and little attempt was made to relate psychological phenomena, and especially the changes in them, to specific historical and social conditions (see above, pp. 21). There was, no doubt, in the later thought of the Frankfurt School, an assumption of growing conformism, brought about by the general rationalization of life and the influence of the 'culture industry'; but this assumption was not tested by any historical or sociological comparative studies, and the social–psychological processes at work were not systematically investigated. Furthermore, the ideas of conformism, assimilation and totalitarianism (a term which Marcuse employs very broadly in *One-Dimensional Man*) are applied in a somewhat uncritical way (by Marcuse more than by Adorno and Horkheimer it should be said) to both capitalist and socialist industrial societies, without a clear recognition of the specific character of the 'actually existing socialism' in Eastern Europe, where conformity to an official ideology is imposed by a dominant party. Even in the case of Eastern Europe the degree of conformism needs to be examined more carefully in the light of the frequent social upheavals, from the revolts of 1953, 1956 and 1968 to the emergence of the 'Solidarity' movement in Poland, and of the virtual extinction of Marxism as a living doctrine (that is, as an effective 'dominant ideology') for a large part of the population in those countries. In the Western capitalist societies there was also a notable eruption of dissent in the late 1960s (which not only led Marcuse to a somewhat more optimistic view of the possibilities of a radical transformation inherent in what he called 'the instinctual refusal among the youth in protest'.[61] but provided a milieu in which the Frankfurt School attained its greatest influence); and today, after a decade of reaction against the ideas of that time, there are substantial and growing manifestations of renewed forms of dissent and protest, in the peace movement, and in the revival of socialism in several countries.

What is required, from a sociological and social–psychological perspective, is a more rigorous account, and if possible an explanation of these cycles of protest and acquiescence, but the Frankfurt School paid scant attention to such matters. To take a particular example: Marcuse's reference to the 'instinctual refusal' of youth seems scarcely adequate, for it provides no clue to the historical fluctuations in the social attitudes of youth, nor does it take account of the very diverse social locations constituted by class, ethnic and national differences; and a much more fruitful line of enquiry in this field seems to be an investigation of the ways in which new 'generations' are formed in particular historical and social circumstances.[62] Marcuse's own reliance upon an instinctual factor derives from his philosophical reinterpretation of Freud in *Eros and Civilization*, which accepts Freud's notion of a universal human nature striving towards the goal of happiness, the latter being defined largely in terms of sexual liberation and gratification, but rejects the view that repression is necessary in order to create and maintain civilization (i.e. that the 'pleasure principle' has to be subordinated to the 'reality principle'). According to Marcuse, the repression of sexuality throughout the history of human society has been primarily 'surplus repression' designed to maintain specific forms of social domination in conditions of economic scarcity; with the end of scarcity this surplus repression can also be ended, and sexual (libidinal) freedom will then transform all other social relationships. Marcuse does not indicate precisely how this transformation will occur, and the experience of greater sexual permissiveness in modern societies suggests that it is easily compatible with continuing economic and class domination. As a whole his philosophical reconstruction of Freud provides little more than speculative, empirically unfounded conceptions of human nature and of the history of civilizations.

The third principal theme in the work of the Frankfurt School – the 'culture industry' – is the one most closely related to sociological concerns. The idea was first propounded, in very sweeping terms, by Horkheimer and Adorno, in their essay 'The culture industry: enlightenment as mass deception',[63] where it was argued that 'under monopoly all mass culture is identical', and at the same time 'depraved' as a consequence of 'the fusion of culture and entertainment'; moreover, there is a merging of advertising and the culture industry, so that both become 'a procedure for manipulating men'. 'The triumph of advertising in the culture industry', they concluded, 'is that consumers feel compelled to buy and use its products even though they see through them' (p. 167). Two features of this account merit attention. In the first place it is difficult, from the essay itself, to grasp exactly how the influence of the culture industry differs from that of cultural domination in other types of society. After all, the Church might well be regarded as the 'culture industry' of medieval Europe. What then is the specific form, in modern capitalist society, of that phenomenon which Marx conceived as the necessary consequence of economic domination, namely that 'the ideas of the ruling class are in every age, the ruling ideas'? Is the present-day culture industry as overwhelmingly effective as is here portrayed, or is Horkheimer's and Adorno's furious denunciation of it to be interpreted, in part at least, as an outcome of the cultural shock produced by their encounter with American commercial radio and television, and the film industry (which, as we have seen, also profoundly affected Marcuse's later account of the ideology of advanced industrial society in *One-Dimensional Man*)?

A consideration of such questions, which point to the need for historical and comparative study of the effects of a 'dominant ideology',[64] raises a second issue; for the strength of an established culture can be measured particularly by the extent of dissent and opposition within the society. Adorno and Horkheimer, in their essay and in later writings, convey the impression that there is no effective dissent, and Marcuse, in *One-Dimensional Man*, presented the same gloomy view. A few years later, however, in the midst of the student rebellion, Marcuse at least was led to revise his judgement, and found some ground for hope in the 'revolt of youth'. It was at this time, in North America especially, that the notion of a 'counter culture' acquired a certain vogue, and Theodore Roszak, in a book which enjoyed a brief notoriety,[65] drew upon the ideas of

Marcuse (though more sympathetically upon those of Norman Brown and Paul Goodman) as constituting 'one of the defining features of the counter culture'. Roszak, like Marcuse, saw the new movement of dissent as a 'youthful opposition' to the technocratic society, but he interpreted it as a 'renaissance of mythical–religious interest', in a way that is somewhat remote from the outlook of the Frankfurt School (though not entirely from Horkheimer's late philosophy) and in particular from that of Marcuse, whose vestigial Marxism he criticized severely.

A major difficulty with the notion of a counter culture is to explain how it could emerge at all in a society dominated so completely by the culture industry. Two solutions are possible: it may be argued either that the limited scope and the rapid disappearance, or assimilation, of the counter culture did in fact reveal the strength of the culture industry; or on the other hand that dissent is actually far more widespread in the capitalist societies of the late twentieth century (and in a more muted but still significant form in the societies of Eastern Europe) than the Frankfurt School recognized, and regularly manifests itself in an upsurge of social and political movements. In the latter case it becomes necessary to give some account of the basis in social life of such dissent and opposition, and here it may be observed that, from a Marxist standpoint, a counter culture has long existed in capitalist society in the form of the socialist movement; a view expressed most vigorously by Gramsci in his conception of the working class movement, with Marxism as its social doctrine, as the bearer of a 'new civilization'. The main issue then becomes that of evaluating the long-term effects, and the historical vicissitudes, of this counter culture embodied in the labour movement. The Frankfurt School itself originated in a specific concern with the failure of the Central European revolutions after the First World War and the rise of National Socialism in Germany, and the ideas of its leading thinkers were further shaped by the consolidation of the Stalinist regime in the USSR and later in Eastern Europe, and by the emergence in the Western capitalist societies after the Second World War (most prominently in the USA) of an apparent political consensus and pacification of major social conflicts, on the basis of exceptional economic growth and more widely diffused prosperity. Their criticism of the state of affairs existing in the 1950s and 1960s directed attention to important and neglected aspects of the postwar development of Western societies (as did the very different social criticism of C. Wright Mills),[66] and in the later 1960s it evoked a strong response among middle class youth, especially in the universities. But in retrospect they may be thought to have exaggerated the degree of conformism and acquiescence in modern societies and the strength of the tendency towards a totalitarian organization of social life, partly at least because of a failure to situate these phenomena in a historical context, or to recognize that contradictory forces have been at work.

It is a fact of considerable importance that in the West European societies during the postwar period socialist and communist parties have increased their membership and their electoral support (though with some fluctuations) to levels never previously achieved; and in this sense it can be claimed that dissent and opposition, historically based upon the working class, are now more widespread than ever before. Against this it may be argued that these parties, and in particular the socialist (or labour, or social democratic) parties, no longer embody a *radical* opposition to the existing form of society, but largely accept its fundamental elements and principles of organization; in short, that they have become purely reformist parties which have abandoned the goal of socialism and a genuinely emancipated society. This is a complex issue,[67] but in the present context we have to consider primarily whether the Frankfurt School thinkers were able to throw fresh light upon it and to provide a plausible account of the main directions of social and cultural change. It is evident that there are major lacunae in their analysis. Thus no reference is made to the actual development of political parties and movements in the postwar period; and this is only an aspect of the unhistorical and non-empirical character of critical theory generally, which results in a failure, on one side, to situate the changing balance between acquiescence and dissent (manifest in the varying intensity of class conflict and other social conflicts) in the long term evolution of capitalism, and on the other side, to investigate in empirical detail the processes of construction and diffusion of ideologies.

A recent study, which examines in a more rigorous and discriminating way the nature and influence of a 'dominant ideology' in late capitalist society, concludes that while the mechanisms of ideological transmission are well developed (by comparison with earlier societies) they are only partly effective; that the extent to which subordinate classes are ideologically incorporated has been exaggerated; and that, to take a particular case, 'Britain is *not* in fact a cohesive society'.[68] The evidence marshalled in this study suggests, at the least, doubts about the omnipotence of the culture industry and about the part that it plays in maintaining domination.

It should be added that in so far as a dominant ideology *is* effective in late capitalist society it derives its strength to a considerable extent from a negative factor; namely, the decline of socialism as a counter culture through its association with the 'actually existing' socialist societies of Eastern Europe (and above all the USSR) in their Stalinist 'totalitarian' and post-Stalinist 'authoritarian' phases.

It is noteworthy that the Frankfurt School thinkers rarely referred to 'socialism' (and then usually in their criticism of Soviet society), and wrote instead of 'emancipation' as the goal of a radical movement. This involved, however, a loss of content and of clarity. Although Marx dismissed the idea of writing 'recipes for the cook-shops of the future' he did in fact give some definite indications of the institutions of a future socialist society in his discussions of cooperative production and in his assessment of the Paris Commune; and in later Marxist and socialist thought the nature and problems of socialism were explored much more fully. The Frankfurt School thinkers ignored this historically formed and diverse body of thought about socialism, and their own ideal of emancipation remained undefined, except in Marcuse's abstract discussion of 'true' and 'false' needs,[69] and in his argument, in *Eros and Civilization*, that sexual liberation and an ensuing transformation of personal relationships are prime elements in the emancipatory process. Whether socialism can be fully reinstated as a persuasive and appealing conception of a new civilization, and what social forces, under what historical conditions, might endow it with a new vitality, is a large and disputed question;[70] but it seems clear that it cannot be adequately explored in the abstract terms of 'emancipation' while disregarding the history of the socialist movement, and its connection with democracy, in the Western capitalist world.

In its mature phase, therefore, the critical theory of the Frankfurt School embodied three interrelated elements: an epistemological and methodological critique of positivism (or more broadly, scientism) in the social sciences; a critical attitude towards the ideological influence of science and technology as a major factor in the creation of a new, technocratic–bureaucratic, form of domination; a preoccupation with the culture industry, and more generally with the cultural aspects of domination. As I have shown, these various elements were not unique to the Frankfurt School, but were closely related to many other currents of European social and philosophical thought in the whole period from the First World War to the 1960s: the continuing, ever-renewed 'revolt against positivism', variously expressed in the Hegelian Marxism of Korsch's and Lukács's early works and in the doctrines of phenomenology and existentialism; the critical attitude to large-scale industrialization, technocracy and bureaucracy formulated by Max Weber in the concept of 'rationalization' and developed in many later sociological writings; the mainly German tradition of cultural criticism which had one important modern source in Tönnies's distinction between *Gemeinschaft* and *Gesellschaft*,[71] and came to influence the Marxism of Lukács and the Frankfurt School particularly through the work of Simmel.

The social–philosophical outlook which suffused all Frankfurt School theory was a 'defence of subjectivity' against the idea of an objective, law-governed process of history; and it was this which evoked an enthusiastic response in the student movement of the 1960s, directed above all against 'the system'. But the New Left and the student movement found inspiration also in a great variety of other Marxist or *marxisant* doctrines, and the influence of the Frankfurt School was notably strongest in those countries where there was no significant indigenous tradition of Marxist thought (Britain and the USA), or where the tradition had been largely eradicated (West Germany). In France and Italy the existence of large Communist parties ensured the persistence of a body of largely orthodox Marxist–Leninist thought, and when this came to be revised, or complemented by new forms of Marxist theory, after 1956, the main intellectual influences were those of Gramsci, Lukács (especially, in France, through the work of Lucien Goldmann), Sartre, and in due course Althusser, who elaborated a new version of Marxism as science. The revisionist Marxism which began to emerge in Eastern Europe at this time was influenced most profoundly by the ideas of Lukács and Gramsci. Finally, the radical social movements of the late 1960s were strongly affected by the Chinese and Cuban revolutions, and by the doctrines of Maoism. The Frankfurt School, therefore, was only one current of thought in a very broad critical renewal of Marxist and radical theories, and its place in the subsequent development of such theories is the subject of much controversy.

NOTES

[1]   Adorno, 'Zur gegenwärtigen Stellung der empirischen Sozialforschung in Deutschland', *Empirische Sozialforschung* (Frankfurt, 1952).

[2]   *Transactions of the Fourth World Congress of Sociology* (London, International Sociological Association, 1959), Vol. I, pp. 38–9.

[3]   As Russell Keat has observed: 'Despite the major significance attached by critical theorists to the critique of positivism, one of the few things that emerges clearly from their work on this is the absence of any clear conception of what positivism consists in'. *The Politics of Social Theory* (Oxford, Basil Blackwell, 1981), p. 12.

[4]   Marcuse, *Reason and Revolution: Hegel and the Rise of Social Theory* (New York: Oxford University Press, 1941), p. 325.

[5]   Horkheimer, 'The Latest Attack on Metaphysics', and 'Traditional and Critical Theory', in *Critical Theory: Selected Essays* (New York, Herder & Herder, 1972).

[6]   See Otto Neurath, 'Unified Science as Encyclopedic Integration', in *Foundations of the Unity of Science*, Otto Neurath, Rudolf Carnap, and Charles Morris (eds), (Chicago, University of Chicago Press, 1969), Vol. I, pp. 1–27.

[7]   Horkheimer, *op. cit.*, p. 183.

[8]   *Ibid.*, pp. 197–8.

[9]   *Ibid.*, pp. 207–8.

[10] *Ibid.*, p. 208.

[11] *Ibid.*, p. 209.

[12] *Ibid.*, p. 210.

[13] *Ibid.*, pp. 140–87. He criticized in particular Otto Neurath's monograph, *Empirical Sociology* (1931; English Translation in *Empiricism and Sociology*, Marie Neurath and Robert S. Cohen (eds), Dordrecht, D. Reidel, 1973), which stated the case for Marxism as 'sociology on a materialist basis', but then went beyond this to expound (very implausibly in my view) what was termed a 'physicalist sociology'.

[14] Horkheimer, *op. cit.*, p. 159.

[15] See especially his paper at the Fourth World Congress of Sociology, 'Contemporary German Sociology' and 'Scientific Experiences of a European Scholar in America', in *The Intellectual Migration: Europe and America, 1930–1960* Donald Fleming and Bernard Bailyn (eds), (Cambridge, Mass., Harvard University Press, 1969).

[16] Adorno, Introduction to *The Positivist Dispute in German Sociology* 1969. (English translation, London, Heinemann, 1976).

[17] As Popper indicated later there was no debate, and his paper was not seriously discussed either at the original conference or in the subsequently published book; see Karl R. Popper, 'Reason or Revolution?', *European Journal of Sociology*, **XI**, 2 (1970).

[18] Adorno, *Negative Dialects* (1966; English translation, New York, Seabury Press, 1973).

[19] The principal studies in English are the highly critical account by Kolakowski, *Main Currents of Marxism* (Oxford, Oxford University Press, 1978), vol. III, pp. 357–69, and Gillian Rose, *The Melancholy Science: An introduction to the Thought of Theodor W. Adorno*, which is also critical, though more sympathetic to Adorno's work as a whole.

[20] See Kolakowski, *loc. cit.*

[21] Marcuse, *Reason and Revolution*, p. 343.

[22] Albrecht Wellmer, *Critical Theory of Society* (New York, Herder & Herder, 1971), chap. 2.

[23] Habermas, *Toward a Rational Society* (Boston, Beacon Press, 1970).

[24] Brian Fay, *Social Theory and Political Practice* (London, Allen & Unwin, 1975).

[25] *Ibid.*, pp. 29–48.

[26] Russell Keat, *The Politics of Social Theory*, p. 21.

[27] Subsequently collected in a volume, *The Counter-Revolution of Science* (Glencoe, The Free Press, 1952).

[28] Hayek notes that they were borrowed from the French; *ibid.*, p. 15.

[29] Fritz Ringer, *The Decline of the German Mandarins* (Cambridge, Mass., Harvard University Press, 1969).

[30] Jay, *The Dialectical Imagination* (Boston, Little, Brown & Co., 1973), p. 294.

[31] Foreword to the new edn of *The Theory of the Novel* (1963; English trans. London, Merlin Press, 1971).

[32] Jay, *op. cit.*, p. 292.

[33] See the latter part of Horkheimer's 'Traditional and Critical Theory'.

[34] Adorno, 'Reflexionen zur Klassentheorie' (1942), in *Gesammelte Schriften* (Frankfurt, Suhrkamp, 1972), Vol. 8, pp. 373–391.

[35] Adorno, 'Gesellschaft' ['Society'], in *Gesammelte Schiften*, Vol. 8, pp. 9–19.

[36] Adorno, 'Spätkapitalismus oder Industriegesellschaft?', in *ibid.*, pp. 354–370.

[37] Marcuse's conception of 'technological rationality' was critically reassessed by the post-Frankfurt School thinkers – notably Habermas and Offe – and their reconstruction of the idea will be examined in the next chapter. See also the discussion in William Leiss, *The Domination of Nature* (New York, George Braziller, 1972), Appendix.

[38] Marcuse, 'Industrialization and Capitalism'.
[39] See the critical comments on this point by Alasdair MacIntyre, *Marcuse* (London, Fontana/Collins, 1970), pp. 67–9.
[40] *Ibid.*, p. 66.
[41] Marcuse, 'Industrialization and Capitalism', p. 179.
[42] *Ibid.*
[43] Wolfgang Mommsen, *The Age of Bureaucracy* (Oxford, Blackwell, 1974), chap. V.
[44] H. Stuart Hughes, *Consciousness and Society* (New York, Alfred A. Knopf, 1958), chap. 2.
[45] A similar influence of the American experience is to be found in C. Wright Mills's dismissal of what he called the 'labour metaphysic' (i.e. the idea of the historical role of the working class) in his essay on 'The New Left', in *Power, Politics and People* (New York, Oxford University Press, 1963), p. 256. On the absence of a socialist movement in the USA see the Introduction to the English translation of Werner Sombart, *Why is there no Socialism in the United States?* (London, Macmillan, 1976), and John H. M. Laslett and Seymour Martin Lipset (eds.), *Failure of a Dream? Essays in the History of American Socialism* (Garden City, New York, Anchor Press/Doubleday, 1974).
[46] See James Burnham, *The Managerial Revolution* (London, Putnam & Co., 1943).
[47] See Georges Gurvitch (ed.), *Industrialisation et technocratie* (Paris, Armand Colin, 1949).
[48] See Raymond Aron, *18 Lectures on Industrial Society* (1961; English translation London, Weidenfeld and Nicolson, 1967), and *The Industrial Society* (1966; English translation London, Weidenfeld and Nicolson 1967); Daniel Bell, *The Coming of Post-Industrial Society* (New York, Basic Books, 1973).
[49] See Alain Touraine, *The Post-Industrial Society* (1969; English translation New York, Random House, 1971), and *The Self-Production of Society* (1973; English translation Chicago, University of Chicago Press, 1977).
[50] On this subject see particularly, George Konrád and Ivan Szelényi, *The Intellectuals on the Road to Class Power* (Brighton, Harvester Press, 1979).
[51] On the economic changes see, for example, the studies of 'monopoly capitalism' and 'state monopoly capitalism' by Keith Cowling, *Monopoly Capitalism* (London, Macmillan, 1982), and Bob Jessop, *The Capitalist State* (Oxford, Martin

Robertson, 1982); see also the analysis of 'advanced capitalism' in Jürgen Habermas, *Legitimation Crisis* (London, Heinemann, 1976). On the diverse analyses of the class structure, see my essays on class collected in *Sociology as Social Criticism* (London, Allen & Unwin, 1975) and in *Sociology and Socialism* (Brighton, Harvester Press, 1984); and also Nicholas Abercrombie and John Urry, *Capital, Labour and the Middle Classes* (London, Allen & Unwin, 1983).

[52] Expressed notably in his reflections on the relevance of Schopenhauer's 'metaphysical pessimism'; see especially the essay on 'Schopenhauers Aktualität', cited in Helmut Gumnior and Rudolf Ringguth, *Max Horkheimer* (Reinbek bei Hamburg, Rowohlt, 1973), final section on Horkheimer's late philosophy.

[53] Preface to *Critical Theory*, p. vii.

[54] See *Die Sehnsucht nach dem ganz Anderen* (an interview with a commentary by Helmut Gumnior; Hamburg, Furche Verlag, 1970).

[55] Gumnior and Ringguth, *op. cit.*, p. 123.

[56] 'Letze Spur von Theologie – Paul Tillichs Vermächtnis'. A talk published in the *Frankfurter Allgemeine Zeitung*, 7 April 1966.

[57] In *Werk und Wirken Paul Tillichs. Ein Gedenkbuch*, p. 16, cited in Gumnior and Ringguth, *op. cit.*, p. 131. For a more extensive discussion of Horkheimer's attitude to religion, and to Judaism and Christianity in particular, see Julius Carlebach, *Karl Marx and the Radical Critique of Judaism* (London, Routledge & Kegan Paul, 1978), pp. 234–57.

[58] Marcuse, *Eros and Civilization* (Boston, Mass., Beacon Press, 1955; new edn with a Political Preface, 1966).

[59] Adorno, *Ästhetische Theorie* (Frankfurt, Suhrkamp, 1970). See also the discussion by the editors in Andrew Arato and Eike Gebhardt (eds), *The Essential Frankfurt School Reader* (New York, Urizen Books, 1978), pp. 185–224.

[60] See, in particular, *Marx's Concept of Man* (New York, Frederick Ungar, 1961), and one of his last works, *The Anatomy of Human Destructiveness* (New York, Holt, Rinehart and Winston, 1973).

[61] See his 'Political Preface' to the 1966 edn of *Eros and Civilization*.

[62] See especially Karl Mannheim's essay 'The Problem of Generations', in *Essays on the Sociology of Knowledge* (London, Rout-

ledge & Kegan Paul, 1952), pp. 276–322; and for an anthropological view, Margaret Mead, *Culture and Commitment: A Study of the Generation Gap* (London, Bodley Head, 1970).

[63]   In *Dialectic of Enlightenment* (New York, Herder & Herder, 1972), pp. 120–67.

[64]   As is admirably undertaken, in a more critical spirit, in Nicholas Abercrombie, Stephen Hill and Bryan S. Turner, *The Dominant Ideology Thesis* (London, Allen & Unwin, 1980).

[65]   Theodore Roszak, *The Making of a Counter Culture* (London, Faber and Faber, 1970).

[66]   See J. E. T. Eldridge, *C. Wright Mills* (Chichester, Ellis Horwood; London and New York, Tavistock Publications, 1983).

[67]   I have examined various aspects of it in an essay on 'The political role of the working class in Western Europe', in Tom Bottomore, *Sociology and Socialism* (Brighton, Harvester Press, 1984).

[68]   Abercrombie, Hill and Turner, *op. cit.*, chap. 5.

[69]   For a more substantial analysis of the concept of 'need' see Agnes Heller, *The Theory of Need in Marx* (London, Alison & Busby, 1976).

[70]   See, for diverse reflections on it, Bhikhu Parekh (ed.), *The Concept of Socialism* (London, Croom Helm, 1975); Leszek Kolakowski and Stuart Hampshire (eds.), *The Socialist Idea: A Reappraisal* (London, Weidenfeld & Nicolson, 1974).

[71]   Ferdinand Tönnies, *Community and Association* (1887; English translation, London, Routledge & Kegan Paul, 1955).

3

Decline and Renewal

With the deaths of Adorno and Horkheimer, and the decline of the radical student movement in the early 1970s, a major phase in the history of the Frankfurt School came to an end. In a sense the school then ceased to exist, certainly as a form of Marxist thought, for its relation to Marxism had become exceedingly tenuous, and it no longer had any connection with political movements. But in another sense it survived, for some of the central ideas of critical theory have continued to influence social thought; with the difference, however, that in the past decade they have been expounded and developed in the works of individual thinkers (above all by Jürgen Habermas, but also, in diverse ways, by Albrecht Wellmer, [1] Alfred Schmidt, [2] and Claus Offe [3]) rather than as part of the research programme of a clearly defined school. At the same time critical theory in its recent development has diverged substantially from some of the main conceptions of Adorno and Horkheimer, while retaining their particular concern with the philosophy of the social sciences and with the critique of ideology.

The writings of Habermas – who is the principal architect of neo-critical theory – fall into two distinct, though not sharply separated, parts. In the first, major part of his work Habermas has pursued the Frankfurt School critique of positivism and has gone on to formulate a new theory of knowledge with particular reference to the social sciences. Thus, in two essays of the 1960s [4] he restates and elaborates some of the objections to positivism (which is conceived, as in the writings of Adorno, Horkheimer and Marcuse, in a very broad and indistinct way, not distinguishing, for example, between nineteenth-century positivism, the logical positivism of the Vienna Circle, Popper's critical rationalism, and modern realism [5]), and contrasts it with a 'dialectical theory'. The latter, he says, 'doubts whether science, with regard to the world produced by men, may proceed just as indifferently as it does with success in the exact natural sciences', because the social sciences have to deal with a pre-constituted reality, with 'the societal life context as a totality which determines even research itself', which remains 'external to the realm of experience analysed'; the dialectical theory employs the concept of 'totality', which refers to a previously understood 'life-world', to be explored by a hermeneutic explication of meaning. Habermas then goes on to criticize the positivist separation of facts and decisions (value choices); that is, the thesis that there are on one side empirical regularities in natural and social phenomena which can be formulated in laws; and on the other side rules of human behaviour, i.e. social norms ('The Analytical Theory of Science and Dialectics', p. 144). The consequence of this dualism is that permissible knowledge is restricted to the empirical sciences, while 'questions of life-practice' are excluded from science, and judgements about social norms rest only on decision; but Habermas goes on to argue that from this standpoint the commitment to science is itself a 'decision', expressed as a 'faith in reason'. [6] His own solution of the 'basis-problem' (i.e. the problem of an empirical testing of theories) is that 'the empirical validity of basic statements, and thereby the plausibility of law-like hypotheses and empirical scientific theories as a whole, is related to the criteria for assessing the results of action which have been socially adopted in the necessarily intersubjective context of working groups. It is here that the hermeneutic pre-understanding . . . is formed, a pre-understanding which first makes possible the application of rules for the acceptance of basic statements. The so-called basis problem simply does not appear if we regard the research process as part of a comprehensive process of socially institutionalised actions, through which social groups sustain their naturally precarious life' (p. 154). At the same time, this solution dissolves the fact/decision dualism, for both scientific judgements and judgements of norms rest upon socially adopted pre-understandings, though not in precisely the same way; as Habermas says in a later work, 'to the truth claims that we raise in empirical statements there correspond claims of correctness or appropriateness that we advance with norms of action or evaluation'. [7]

Following these critical essays Habermas formulated, in *Knowledge and Human Interests*, [8] a new theory of knowledge which – departing radically from Adorno's scepticism – would establish secure foundations for knowledge by connecting it with basic interests of the human species. Three forms of knowledge are distinguished, resting upon three knowledge-constitutive interests: (i) a 'technical' interest grounded in material needs and labour, which constitutes the object-domain of empirical–analytic science; (ii) a 'practical' interest in communicative understanding between individuals and within or between social groups, grounded in the species-universal characteristic of language, which constitutes the domain of historical–hermeneutic knowledge; and (iii) an 'emancipatory' interest, grounded in the distorted actions and utterances resulting from the exercise of power, which constitutes the domain of self-reflective or critical knowledge. Habermas's conception of object-constitution is, as Keat notes, partly Kantian, but he differs from Kant (and also from the neo-Kantian Austro-Marxist view and the modern realist philosophy of science) [9] in arguing that 'the necessary features of these objects . . . cannot be derived by transcendental arguments establishing the conditions for the possibility of knowledge for any knowing subject, but instead must be seen to result from a particular interest of the human species that is grounded in a species-universal characteristic'. [10]

The argument in *Knowledge and Human Interests* is still directed primarily against positivism, or more generally against 'scientism'; that is, against the replacement of the theory of knowledge 'by a methodology emptied of philosophical thought. For the philosophy of science that has emerged since the mid-nineteenth century as the heir of the theory of knowledge is methodology pursued with a scientistic self-understanding of the sciences. "Scientism" means science's belief in itself: that is, the conviction that we can no longer understand science as one form of possible knowledge, but rather must identify knowledge with science' (p. 4). Habermas's differentiation of three forms of knowledge, alike rooted in human interests, whose validity-claims have to be tested in a similar way by rational argument, and if upheld are sustained by a rational agreement among the members of a community, is intended to deny the claims of empirical–analytic science to 'exclusive validity', and at the same time to overcome the dichotomy of fact and decision.

The theory of knowledge formulated in *Knowledge and Human Interests* (which has been substantially modified, if not abandoned, in Habermas's later work, as we shall see) provoked extensive discussion and criticism, [11] which I shall attempt to summarize with due regard to the difficulty of expounding briefly the issues raised by a body of thought which is itself complex, opaque, and far from being characterized by succinctness of expression. First, Habermas's conception of three forms of knowledge based upon knowledge-constitutive interests was questioned from several aspects. The distinction between empirical–analytic science and historical–hermeneutic knowledge has seemed to some critics to reproduce the long established contrast in German social thought between 'explanation' and 'understanding', regarded as differentiating the methods of the natural sciences from those of the social and cultural sciences. This may not have been Habermas's intention, but he gives no precise indication of how (or whether) the two kinds of knowledge come together in social science theories; [12] whether, that is, there are causal chains in social life which can be brought within the explanatory scheme of an empirical–analytic science, as well as phenomena which have to be hermeneutically 'understood'. Habermas's third knowledge-constitutive interest – the emancipatory interest – has been regarded sceptically by many critics, who see it as being much less clearly defined than the other two interests and forms of knowledge, or indeed, in Kolakowski's view, as being no more than another (unsuccessful) attempt, in the tradition of German idealism, to transcend the opposition between practical and theoretical reason, cognition and will. [13] Habermas's attempt to present psychoanalysis as 'the only tangible example of a science incorporating methodical self-reflection', [14] hence 'emancipatory', has been examined in some detail by Keat, [15] who argues that the exegesis of Freud's theory by Habermas involves such a degree of misinterpretation as to cast serious doubt upon the use of psychoanalysis as a model for critical social theory, and goes on to propose an alternative view of psychoanalytic theory (closer to Freud's own conception) as involving causal explanation, which still allows, within limits, emancipation in the sense of greater autonomy.

Habermas's theory of knowledge also raises some more general problems. The theory of truth which is involved in it is a 'consensus' theory, and Habermas firmly opposes any 'correspondence' theory, which would, in his view, bolster the 'false objectivism' of the positivist philosophy of science. But this poses the question of whether a consensus theory does adequately describe or account for the actual procedures of the natural sciences, or indeed of the social sciences; whether, that is, the 'truth' that is attained by scientific enquiry can properly be conceived only as an agreement reached by rational argument, or in other ways, in a community of scientists, a closed meaning-system not involving any reference to its correspondence with an external reality. [16] A major difficulty with Habermas's exposition is that he does not discuss specific cases of the testing of validity-claims by argument, or how agreement is (or is not) eventually reached, and in particular does not confront, in terms of the history of science, the question of how choices are made among competing theories, or on the other hand, whether there are 'incommensurable' theories. And this suggests a larger question about the fruitfulness, for the social sciences, of the attempt to establish an ultimate basis of knowledge – a 'first philosophy' – as against the more modest aim of a philosophy of science which proceeds from the body of acquired knowledge to an enquiry into the transcendental conditions for the possibility of such knowledge.

At all events, in his work over the past decade Habermas appears to have revised substantially the doctrine expounded in *Knowledge and Human Interests*. In his reply to critics, commenting on a criticism of his 'first philosophy', he refers to his 'renunciation of ultimate foundations, be they of a traditional or of a critical sort', and in the same passage he also observes that 'the coherence theory of truth is certainly too weak to explain the concept of propositional truth', but argues that 'it comes into its own at another level, the metatheoretical, where we put together the individual pieces of theory like a puzzle'. [17] The idea of knowledge-constitutive interests now seems to be abandoned, or at least disregarded, and what is presented instead is a theory of language and communication, which is both a theory of truth and at the same time a doctrine of emancipation. The importance of language was stated earlier by Habermas, in his inaugural lecture of 1965, where he argued that 'what raises us out of nature is the only thing whose nature we can know: language. Through its structure autonomy and responsibility are posited for us. Our first sentence expresses unequivocally the intention of universal and unconstrained consensus'; [18] and in *Zur Logik der Sozialwissenschaft* [19] where he formulated as a major element in critical theory 'the idea of a communication free from domination'. But in his more recent writing it has come to occupy a central place in a reformulated consensus theory of truth. In his reply to critics Habermas cites as an adequate summary of his theoretical programme the following passage from McCarthy: 'Claims to truth and rightness, if radically challenged, can be redeemed only through argumentative discourse leading to rationally motivated consensus. Universal–pragmatic analysis of the conditions of discourse and rational consensus show these to rest on the supposition of an "ideal speech situation" characterized by an effective equality of chances to assume dialogue roles'; [20] and he then goes on to consider 'the problem of what it means to redeem validity-claims discursively; this problem calls for an investigation of the communicative presuppositions of argumentative speech (discourse theory of truth) and an analysis of the general procedural rules of argumentation (logic of discourse)'.[21]

The same objections can be levelled against this theory of truth as were brought against the conception of truth embedded in Habermas's earlier theory of knowledge. First, the 'consensus' theory that is maintained here (although, as we have seen, Habermas does seem to qualify it with respect to propositional truth, but without fully explicating his position) may be held to misrepresent the actual practice of the sciences in so far as this involves recourse to some notion of correspondence with reality. Second, it may be argued that it is less fruitful and enlightening to adopt, as Habermas does, a 'universalization' thesis, than to analyse in a more discriminating way the differences between science and non-science, between pure and practical reason, between the validity-claims and the ways of questioning and redeeming them that are characteristic of the natural sciences, the social sciences, and moral or aesthetic judgements.[22] The basic intention of the 'universalization thesis' is still, as in Habermas's earlier work, to bring together in a single notion of 'truth' both factual and normative judgements; but this, in my view, obscures the very great differences in the forms of reasoning and in the strength of validity-claims (that is, the degree to which they can be effectively redeemed by argument) in different spheres. From this perspective it can be argued that knowledge *is*, in an important sense, identical with science; that the natural sciences provide a model of reliable knowledge, that the scientific status of the social sciences remains problematic in certain respects because of the nature of the realm of facts with which they deal, and that normative questions, in the spheres of social, political and cultural life, are only in part matters of knowledge (to the extent that normative judgements are influenced by beliefs about factual states of affairs) and involve, beyond that, value-orientations to the world dependent upon sentiments which may in turn be related to social

interests and personality traits. Hence the notoriously greater difficulty in resolving moral or aesthetic disagreements, as compared
with those which arise in science, through any kind of 'argumentative discourse'. Habermas pays altogether too little attention to
these differences, and this is connected with the fact (already mentioned with regard to his theory of knowledge) that he presents his
theory in a formal and abstract way, rather than incorporating in
the exposition some exemplary analyses of the ways in which specific
validity-claims are actually challenged and redeemed in the different
spheres of discourse – as is customary, for example, in discussions of
the philosophy of science and in many studies of moral or aesthetic
theory. This is to say that he does not confront, directly and
explicitly, the crucial question of how specific judgemental or
theoretical disagreements are, or might be, resolved.

In Habermas's most recent work – the massive two-volume
exposition of a 'theory of communicative action' [23] – there is again
a significant change in the focus of attention, but with an underlying
continuity of thought represented by the retention of the 'universalization thesis'. Habermas's aim, as he explains in the introduction
(p. 23), is: (i) to explicate the concept of rationality; (ii) to incorpo-
rate the concept in an evolutionary view of the emergence of a
modern comprehension of the world; and (iii) to show the internal
connection between the theory of rationality and the theory of society, at both a meta-theoretical and a methodological level. Here,
Habermas's philosophical concerns merge with the second part of
his work – the construction of a theory of society – and the book is
largely devoted to an analysis and assessment of diverse conceptions
of rationalization and modernization in social theory. In Volume I
Max Weber's theory of the rationalization of the modern world is
examined in great detail, and this is followed by a critical account of
later developments of the theory, from Lukács's use of the concept of
reification to Horkheimer's and Adorno's critique of instrumental
reason. Then in Volume II Habermas undertakes a critique of 'functionalist reason' as it appears in the work of Mead and Durkheim, in
hermeneutic interpretations of the 'life world', and in the systems
theory of Talcott Parsons. He concludes by outlining the present
tasks of a critical theory of society – requiring in his view a retracing
of steps from Parsons, via Weber, to Marx – which I shall discuss in
the next chapter.

There has always been, of course, a connection in Habermas's
thought between philosophical analysis and a theory of society, but
its nature has gradually changed. At the time of *Knowledge and*

Human Interests (1974) it appeared that the theory of knowledge was based upon a social theory, the three forms of knowledge corresponding with three basic features of social life, namely labour, interaction and domination; but in the following period the attempt to formulate a theory of knowledge seems to be given up, and Habermas propounds a theory of truth which is rooted, not in society, but in language as a universal species characteristic.[24] This idea continues to play a part in Habermas's recent work, but there is now a much stronger emphasis upon the construction (or reconstruction) of a theory of society.

This already marks a significant departure from the outlook of the Frankfurt School in its last phase, and the divergence is made more explicit by Habermas's declaration that he approaches social theory as a 'Marxist theoretician', concerned to 'carry on the Marxian tradition under considerably changed historical conditions'.[25] The elements of a reconstructed Marxist theory are set out in two important works of the 1970s, on the problems of legitimation in late capitalist societies [26] and on historical materialism.[27] In the first of these texts, after elucidating his concept of crisis in a social system, which draws upon Marx (who 'developed, for the first time, a social scientific concept of system crisis') and upon modern systems theory, Habermas goes on to present a descriptive model of advanced capitalism and to distinguish four principal 'crisis tendencies'; namely, economic crisis, rationality crisis, legitimation crisis, and motivation crisis (*Legitimation Crisis*, pp. 33–94). The central theme of Habermas's analysis is a reassessment of 'the chances for a self-transformation of advanced capitalism', a question which he sees 'no possibility of cogently deciding' (p. 40), because of the uncertainty about whether economic crisis can be permanently averted, and if so, whether this could only be done in such a way as to produce other crisis tendencies. The main features of advanced capitalism that create this uncertainty are, on one side, the extent of state intervention in the economy, and on the other, the decline of class conflict, which 'the most advanced capitalist countries have succeeded . . . in keeping . . . latent in its decisive areas', so that 'class compromise . . . has become part of the structure of advanced capitalism' and 'class consciousness is fragmented' (pp. 38–9). In the light of these circumstances Habermas gives prominence, throughout the rest of his analysis, to the non-economic crisis tendencies, particularly those in the spheres of legitimation and motivation, and he tentatively summarizes a complex argument in the following way: 'Because the economic system has forfeited its functional autonomy *vis à vis* the state, crisis manifestations in advanced capitalism have also lost their nature-like character . . . (and) a system crisis is not to be expected . . . Economic crises are shifted into the political system . . . in such a way that supplies of legitimation can compensate for deficits in rationality and extensions of organizational rationality can compensate for those legitimation deficits that do appear. There arises a bundle of crisis tendencies . . . The less the cultural system is capable of producing adequate motivations for politics, the educational system, and the occupational system, the more must scarce meaning be replaced by consumable values . . . The definitive limits to procuring legitimation are inflexible normative structures that no longer provide the economic–political system with ideological resources, but instead confront it with exorbitant demands' (pp. 92–3).

Other scholars associated with the Frankfurt Institute, and with the Max-Planck Institut in Starnberg (where Habermas was Director of Research from 1972 to 1981), have taken up similar problems for study. Thus Offe, in the work mentioned earlier, *Industry and Inequality*, undertakes a critique of the 'achievement principle' as a major legitimating principle in advanced capitalist society – that is, as 'a model of society in which social status is distributed equitably in line with performance' (p. 134) – and endeavours to show that its consequences conflict with existing interests and values; with the result that its validity 'is becoming factually debatable and its claim to validity is revealed as politically and morally untenable' (p. 137). In other works,[28] Offe has examined the role of the state and the nature of political power in late capitalist societies, and has argued broadly that in this type of society 'any attempt to explain the political organization of power through the categories of political economy becomes implausible. That is to say, *both* sides of the politically represented class relationship, [i.e. ruling class and subordinate class] become problematic . . .'[29] The general conception of political organization in late capitalist societies at which Offe arrives is that of 'corporatism'; a system in which the state, in order to maintain the existing order and deal with threats to stability, negotiates agreements with large capital and organized labour, thus establishing a 'class compromise'.[30]

The emphasis, in the social theory of the neo-critical theorists, upon the changed political significance of social classes, and still more the preoccupation with questions of legitimation and motivation, indicate some continuity with the ideas of the earlier Frankfurt School. But there are also profound differences. Habermas and those who have been influenced by his work take Marx's thought more explicitly and deliberately as their starting point, and conceive their task as a reconstruction of Marxist theory, not its supersession. Hence their account of social classes is not presented in terms of an alleged total incorporation of the working class into late capitalist society, but in terms of the 'latency' of class conflict, and Habermas explicitly formulates as one of the questions which a theory of advanced capitalism must attempt to clarify: 'in what crisis tendencies does the temporarily suppressed, but unresolved class antagonism express itself?' [31] Similarly, in examining the significance of legitimation and motivation in the maintenance of domination they do not adopt the standpoint of an exclusively cultural critique, nor can they be considered as propounding a very strong version of the 'dominant ideology thesis',[32] for their studies of the crisis tendencies in capitalist society are set firmly in the framework of a prior analysis of the economic and political structures of late capitalism. Nevertheless, it may be argued that there is still, in this more recent work, too strong an emphasis upon questions of ideology and legitimation, an inadequate account of the development of social classes and class conflict, and an underestimation of the possibility of a purely or predominantly, economic crisis; and I shall examine these larger issues in the next chapter.

Habermas's second major contribution to a theory of society also indicates plainly the more direct involvement of the neo-critical theorists with Marxism. His project of 'reconstructing' historical materialism, he says, 'signifies taking a theory apart and putting it back together again in a new form in order to attain more fully the goal it has set for itself. This is the normal way (in my opinion normal for Marxists too) of dealing with a theory that needs revision in many respects but whose potential for stimulation has still not been exhausted'.[33] The reconstruction, however, does involve very drastic revisions, and Habermas himself indicates a possible objection to his project by posing the question of why one should 'insist any longer on the *Marxist* theoretical tradition', when 'the investigation of the capitalist accumulation process, on which Marx concentrated above all, hardly plays a role in the reformulation of the basic assumptions regarding social evolution'. In response, he argues that 'the anatomy of bourgeois society is a key to the anatomy of premodern societies' and 'to this extent the analysis of capitalism provides an excellent entry into the theory of evolution', because 'the general concept of a principle of social organization can be discerned in capitalist societies' as a result of the emergence of class structure in a pure form, a model of the generation of crises can be developed, and 'the mechanism of legitimating domination can be grasped in bourgeois ideologies'. Hence he concludes that 'the constitutive features of this mode of production (capitalism) are also instructive for social formations in earlier stages'. Nevertheless, he continues, 'from this one cannot derive a demand that "the logic of capital" be utilized as the key to the logic of social evolution'; and by way of illustration he argues that '*if* a socialist organization of society *were* the adequate response to crisis-ridden developments in capitalist society, it could not be deduced from any "determination of the form" of the reproductive process, but would have to be explained in terms of processes of democratization; that is, in terms of the penetration of universalistic structures into action domains which . . . were previously reserved to the private autonomous setting of ends'.[34]

The central element (apparent in the passages just cited) in Habermas's reconstruction of historical materialism is the distinction he has made since his earliest work between 'labour' and 'interaction' (or 'communicative action'). Thus he begins his reformulation of Marx's theory by examining the basic concept of social labour, or socially organized labour, as 'the specific way in which humans, in contradistinction to animals, reproduce their lives'. This concept, he suggests, does not adequately characterize the form of reproduction of human life: 'it cuts too deeply into the evolutionary scale; not only humans but hominids too were distinguished from the anthropoid apes in that they converted to reproduction through social labour and developed an economy' (p. 134). Hence the concept needs to be supplemented, in order to capture the specifically human reproduction of life, by another which recognizes that 'humans were the first to break up the social structure that arose with the vertebrates', through the establishment of a familial social structure requiring a system of social norms that presupposed language (p. 136). This is not a total departure from the view formulated by Marx, who wrote in the *German Ideology* (Introduction) that 'This mode of production should not be regarded simply as the reproduction of the physical existence of individuals. It is already a definite form of activity of these individuals, a definite way of expressing their life, a definite *mode of life*'.[35] There is some divergence, however, for Habermas's claim is that the origin and development of specifically human life depends upon two elements – social labour and language – which are irreducible to each other, whereas Marx, although he did not discuss questions of linguistic theory at any length, seems to assert the unity of material–social activity and language, and Engels (as well as Lukács subsequently) argued that language originates from work.[36]

Even if social labour and language are conceived as irreducible elements the question arises as to whether one of them has greater significance in explaining the historical development of human society. Here Habermas appears to remain close to Marx's conception, for he summarizes his view by saying, first, that: 'The concept of social labour is fundamental, because the evolutionary achievement of socially organized labour and distribution obviously precedes the emergence of developed linguistic communication, and this in turn precedes the development of social role systems' (p. 137). But he then qualifies this by observing that we also need the concept of familial organization for an adequate description of the human mode of life; that rules of communicative action (i.e. norms of action) cannot be reduced to rules of instrumental action; and finally that since 'production and socialization, social labour and care for the young, are equally important for the reproduction of the species', the familial social structure, which controls both aspects, is fundamental (p. 138).

In another respect, however, Habermas does stay close to Marx's theory, for in elucidating the concept of a 'history of the species' and Marx's distinctive conception of history as a discrete series of modes of production, he apparently accepts the broad framework of this periodization of history, only rejecting a dogmatic version which would imply a unilinear, necessary, uninterrupted and invariably progressive development (more Stalinist than Marxist, for Marx had already introduced many qualifications, notably in his discussion of pre-capitalist economic formations in the *Grundrisse*). But in this case the mode of production remains the crucial feature in defining historical periods and forms of society, whereas it might have been expected that Habermas's insistence upon the *equal* importance of social labour and familial organization (implying norms of conduct) would lead to some more substantial revision of Marx's scheme. Otherwise, it is difficult to see what real difference in the interpretation of social development is achieved by this reconstruction of historical materialism, except with regard to the *future*; that is, the possibility of a transition from capitalism to socialism which, as I noted earlier, Habermas regards as depending more upon processes of democratization than upon changes in the mode of production. The restricted character of Habermas's 'reconstruction' I would interpret mainly as a consequence of his disregard of the work of historians, and this raises a larger question about the place of historical studies in Frankfurt School and neo-critical theory which I shall consider in the next chapter.

It would be difficult, if not impossible, to sum up at this stage the substantive achievement and the influence of Habermas's work, not least because his conceptions are evidently still developing and have already undergone significant changes. What is most apparent, I think, is the extent to which he has diverged from the ideas of the earlier Frankfurt School. In a sense he has retraced, in reverse, the path followed by Adorno and Horkheimer, assigning much greater importance to a distinctively Marxist theory of society; hence he has devoted more attention to the analysis of economic and political structures, while conversely, there is very little reference in his work to the 'culture industry'. Further, he does not, to the same extent, identify critical theory with philosophical thought, in opposition to science. Critique, he suggests, has to be located in some way 'between philosophy and science,'[37] and this conception provides room for an empirical science of society, although this would not exhaust the possibility of social knowledge and would be complemented, or situated in the framework of, 'a philosophy of history with political intent'.[38]

At the same time, there are some obvious continuities in critical theory from the 1930s to the present time. Although Habermas does not assign to philosophy quite the pre-eminent role that it came to have in the thought of Adorno and Horkheimer, it is undoubtedly the case that in his earlier work particularly he was still largely preoccupied with the critique of positivism, and his influence has so far been most strongly marked in metatheoretical debates about the philosophical foundations of the social sciences; only more recently, in his own work and in the research programme of the Starnberg Institute, has the reconstruction of social theory itself come to occupy a more prominent place. But in this sphere, too, there are elements of continuity, notably in the kind of attention given to the changing situation and role of social classes in late capitalist society, as a major problem for Marxist theory, and to Weber's conception of the increasing rationalization of social life as embodying a view of the main tendencies of capitalist development which is an alternative or complement to Marx's analysis. These are among the most important questions to be investigated in the next chapter.

NOTES

[1]   Albrecht Wellmer, *Critical Theory of Society* (New York, Herder and Herder, 1971); see also his recent reflections on critical theory, in 'Reason, Utopia, and the Dialectic of Enlightenment', *Praxis International,* **3**(2), July 1983.

[2]   Alfred Schmidt, *The Concept of Nature in Marx* (London, New Left Books, 1971) and *Die Kritische Theorie als Geschichtsphilosophie* (Munich, Carl Hanser, 1976).

[3]   Claus Offe, *Strukturprobleme des Kapitalistischen Staates* (Frankfurt, Suhrkamp, 1972); *Industry and Inequality* (London, Edward Arnold, 1976).

[4]   Habermas, 'The Analytical Theory of Science and Dialectics' and 'A Positivistically Bisected Rationalism', in Adorno *et al.,* *The Positivist Dispute in German Sociology,* pp. 131–62, 198–225.

[5]   See the very pertinent comments of Hans Albert, 'A Short and Surprised Postscript to a Long Introduction', in *The Positivist Dispute in German Sociology,* pp. 283–7.

[6]   As Max Weber also intimated in 'Science as a vocation', and more generally in his distinction between different 'value spheres'; see Rogers Brubaker, *The Limits of Rationality: An Essay on the Social and Moral Thought of Max Weber* (London, Allen & Unwin, 1984).

[7]   Habermas, *Legitimation Crisis* (London, Heinemann, 1976), p. 10.

[8]   Habermas, *Knowledge and Human Interests* (London, Heinemann, 1972).

[9]   For the Austro-Marxist conception, see the texts of Max Adler translated in Bottomore and Goode, *Austro-Marxism* (Oxford, Oxford University Press, 1978), Part II; for the realist conception, see Roy Bhaskar, *A Realist Theory of Science* (2nd edn, Brighton, Harvester Press, 1978) and *The Possibility of Naturalism* (Brighton, Harvester Press, 1979), and also Russell Keat and John Urry, *Social Theory as Science* (Postscript to 2nd edn, London, Routledge & Kegan Paul, 1982).

[10]   Keat, *The Politics of Social Theory* (Oxford, Basil Blackwell, 1981), p. 5. Keat provides, in the introduction and in Chap. 3, an excellent summary of Habermas's theory, and in chaps. 4–5 an assessment of Habermas's use of psychoanalysis as a model for critical theory.

[11]   See especially Thomas McCarthy, *The Critical Theory of Jürgen Habermas* (London, Hutchinson, 1978) and Keat, *The Politics*

of Social Theory; and for more recent critical assessments, with a reply by Habermas, John B. Thompson and David Held (eds), *Habermas: Critical Debates* (London, Macmillan, 1982).

[12] Habermas regards natural science as involving only empirical–analytic knowledge and rejects the idea of a 'hermeneutics of nature', which Keat criticizes as an internal inconsistency in his position (*op. cit.*, pp. 78–84).

[13] Kolakowski, *Main Currents of Marxism* (Oxford, Oxford University Press, 1968), vol. III, pp. 393–4.

[14] Habermas, *Knowledge and Human Interests*, p. 214.

[15] Keat, *The Politics of Social Theory*.

[16] This is a large and complex question, the subject of extensive controversy in recent philosophy of science, which cannot be pursued here. Many of the alternative views and disagreements about 'testability', 'falsification', and the 'theory-dependence' of observation statements emerge clearly in the collection of papers edited by Imre Lakatos and Alan Musgrave, *Criticism and the Growth of Knowledge* (Cambridge, Cambridge University Press, 1970), and are broadly reviewed in T. S. Kuhn's contribution, 'Reflections on my Critics' (pp. 231–78). See also, for a concise summary of the main points at issue, Michael Mulkay, *Science and the Sociology of Knowledge* (London, Allen & Unwin, 1979).

[17] In Thompson and Held (eds), *Habermas: Critical Debates*, p. 239.

[18] Published as an appendix to *Knowledge and Human Interests*.

[19] *Zur Logik der Sozialwissenschaften* (Frankfurt, Suhrkamp, 1970).

[20] McCarthy, *The Critical Theory of Jürgen Habermas*, p. 325.

[21] Thompson and Held, *op. cit.*, p. 256.

[22] As is essayed, for example, with respect to the difference between natural and social science, in Bhaskar, *The Possibility of Naturalism*.

[23] Habermas, *Theorie des kommunikativen Handelns* (2 vols, Frankfurt, Suhrkamp, 1981).

[24] See on this question McCarthy's discussion of Habermas's defence of rationality against relativism, in Thompson and Held, *op. cit.*, pp. 57–78; and on the general issue of relativism, Martin Hollis and Steven Lukes (eds), *Rationality and Relativism* (Oxford, Blackwell, 1982).

[25] In his reply to Agnes Heller; see Thompson and Held, *op. cit.*, p. 220.

[26] Habermas, *Legitimation Crisis* (London, Heinemann, 1976).

[27] Habermas, *Zur Rekonstruktion des Historischen Materialismus* (Frankfurt, Suhrkamp, 1976). The introduction and the central chapter on historical materialism have been translated in Habermas, *Communication and the Evolution of Society* (London, Heinemann, 1979), pp. 95–129, 130–76.

[28] Claus Offe, *Strukturprobleme des kapitalistischen Staates* (Frankfurt, Suhrkamp, 1972), and 'Political Authority and Class Structures – An Analysis of Late Capitalist Societies', *International Journal of Sociology*, **ii**, 1 (1972).

[29] Offe, 'Political Authority . . .', p. 81.

[30] Offe, 'The Separation of Form and Content in Liberal Democratic Politics', *Studies in Political Economy*, **3** (1980). See also Leo Panitch, 'The Development of Corporatism in Liberal Democracies', *Comparative Political Studies*, **10** (1977); and the entry 'Crisis in Capitalist Society' in Tom Bottomore (ed.), *A Dictionary of Marxist Thought* (Oxford, Blackwell, 1983).

[31] *Legitimation Crisis*, p. 39.

[32] For a discussion of Habermas's work in relation to this thesis see Abercrombie, Hill and Turner, *op. cit.*, pp. 15–20.

[33] *Communication and the Evolution of Society*, p. 95

[34] *Ibid.*, pp. 123–4.

[35] See also the comment by Wellmer (*Critical Theory of Society*, p. 67) to the effect that when Marx speaks of production he also means 'forms of intercourse', which corresponds to 'communicative behaviour'. Wellmer goes on to argue, however, that in Marx's theory of history there is a latent positivistic misconception of the self-production of the human species as involving only labour and the production of objects.

[36] See the entry 'Linguistics', in Tom Bottomore (ed.) *A Dictionary of Marxist Thought*.

[37] Habermas, *Theory and Practice* (London, Heinemann, 1974), chap. 6, 'Between Philosophy and Science: Marxism as Critique'. This chapter, first published in 1968, also contains a clear statement of Habermas's view, at that time, of the major deficiencies of Marxist theory in relation to the development of capitalism.

[38] *Ibid.*, p. 242.

Conclusion: A Critical Assessment of the Critics

In the preceding chapters I have outlined the principal ideas and themes of the Frankfurt School during its different phases, and in the course of doing so indicated some of the criticisms which have been, or can be, directed against it on particular issues. But this account needs to be complemented by a more general assessment of the school's contribution to the development of Marxist thought and sociological theory over the past half century.

One striking feature of its work, which has been insufficiently remarked, is that in spite of the original aim of the Frankfurt Institute to promote interdisciplinary research the range of its interests became in fact extremely limited. In the first place we should note that after the early years of the Institute's existence, when Carl Grünberg was its director, historical studies played no part in its work and no historian was closely associated with its activities. This disregard of history was intimately connected with the conception that the Frankfurt School, as it took shape under the influence of Adorno and Horkheimer, had of social theory, as being only, or primarily, a critique of the present time. Of course, this bore some relation to Marx's view, at least as it was expressed in his earliest and most Hegelian writings; for example, in his letter to Ruge, published in the *Deutsch-Französische Jahrbücher* (1844), where he describes the aim of the new journal as being to 'develop new principles for the world out of the principles of the world . . . show the world why it actually struggles . . . (and) *explain* to the world its own acts', thus attaining 'a self-understanding (critical philosophy) of the age concerning its struggle and desires'. It is also the case that in his subsequent work Marx devoted by far the greater part of his attention to an analysis of modern capitalist society, but from the time of the *German Ideology* he set this analysis firmly within a 'science of history', the elements of which are clearly indicated in several texts, on the origins and development of capitalism, on pre-capitalist economic formations, and on early societies.

The Frankfurt School idea of theory was much closer to that of Korsch – by which it was originally influenced – who conceived Marxism, in Marx's own early Young Hegelian fashion, as a 'critical philosophy', the 'theoretical expression of the revolutionary movement of the proletariat'[1] This posed crucial difficulties later, as we shall see, in defining the status of 'critical theory' in the apparent absence of a revolutionary proletariat. For the present, however, I want to concentrate on the general consequences of the Frankfurt School's unhistorical approach. One of these was that the School tended to be excessively influenced in its social analysis by immediate and sometimes ephemeral phenomena, which were not systematically investigated from a historical and comparative perspective. This is apparent in the nature of their preoccupation with National Socialism and anti-Semitism in the 1930s and 1940s, with the 'culture industry' in the 1950s, and perhaps most of all in Marcuse's espousal in the 1960s of the idea that diverse social movements – among students, ethnic minorities, and in the Third World – constituted the elements of a new 'revolutionary subject' of history. It is equally evident in the Frankfurt School thinkers' ultimate rejection of the fundamental Marxist notion of the working class as a revolutionary force in capitalist society, without any investigation of the actual historical development of the working class and of working class movements and parties, or any attempt to compare, for example, the situation of the bourgeoisie as a revolutionary class in feudal society with that of the working class in advanced capitalism.

The Frankfurt School, that is to say, made no attempt to reassess Marx's theory of history as a whole, and indeed simply ignored it. With the recent work of Habermas, however, a change has taken place; and his 'reconstruction of historical materialism' is intended, as I showed in the previous chapter, to reformulate the theory in a more adequate form. But this attempt too is curiously unhistorical in its approach, and is largely confined to conceptual analysis, although some attention is given to recent work by anthropologists and prehistorians bearing upon the origins of human societies, and there are brief references to the debates about the Asiatic mode of production and about the categorization of feudalism. What is required, however, for any substantial reassessment of Marx's theory, is a thorough reconsideration of the historical evidence relating to the structure of, and processes of change within, the major forms of society.[2] At the same time we have to ask what differences in the interpretation of historical change would result from the acceptance of Habermas's fundamental principle that the constitution and development of human societies has to be conceived in terms of two distinct and mutually irreducible processes: labour (or instrumental action) and communicative action. What modifications, if any, would this necessitate, for example, in Marxist studies (or those strongly influenced by Marxism) of the rise of capitalism; such as Braudel's massive and comprehensive account of *Civilization and Capitalism*,[3] or the diverse and contested views expounded in a recent series of essays in *Past and Present*?[4] It is not at all clear how this question might be answered, and in my view we have to recognize that detailed historical research is at least as important as sociological analysis and conceptual clarification for any adequate reconstruction of Marx's theory of history, or for transcending it in a new theory.

Just as the Frankfurt School thinkers neglected, or excluded, history, so also they largely ignored economic analysis. It was in the early years of the Institute that economic theorists (like historians) were most prominent; and notably Henryk Grossmann, whose study of capitalist accumulation and breakdown[5] was published in 1929 as the first volume in a series of publications by the Institute. But Grossmann, as Jay remarks, can 'scarcely be described as a major force in [the School's] intellectual development', since he was largely unsympathetic to the dialectical, neo-Hegelian approach which came to dominate its work.[6] The major economic theorist associated with the Institute at a later stage was Franz Neumann, but his association was brief, and like Grossmann he was unsympathetic to critical theory. The only economist who occupied a central place in the Frankfurt School was Horkheimer's close friend Friedrich Pollock, and his work – on Soviet planning, and later on automation – dealt primarily with questions of economic policy. The school as such devoted little attention to a theoretical or historical analysis of the development of the capitalist economy, and produced no study that is at all comparable with Hilferding's writings on 'finance capital' and 'organized capitalism',[7] or with Neumann's analysis of the relation between 'monopoly capitalism' and the National Socialist regime.[8]

Again this situation has changed to some extent with the work of the neo-critical theorists. Habermas, in the 'descriptive model of advanced capitalism' which he outlines in *Legitimation Crisis* (Part II, chap. 1), and in a following chapter (chap. 4) on economic crisis, discusses briefly some aspects of the capitalist economy, while Offe, in *Strukturprobleme des kapitalistischen Staates*, likewise refers to the economic characteristics of advanced capitalism. But their attention is concentrated on the role of the 'interventionist state', and on the related problems of legitimation; and they do not attempt either a theoretical analysis of the capitalist mode of production in its latest phase, or a historical depiction of its development. Moreover, it is still the case that no major economic theorist is associated with critical theory, even in its revised form, and the school as a whole has never made a significant contribution to Marxist economic theory as it developed through the work of Hilferding and later thinkers.[9]

The neglect of historical research on one side, and of economic analysis on the other, separates the Frankfurt School and its prolongation in neo-critical theory very sharply from Marxism. But the most obvious divergence from what may be called in broad terms 'classical' Marxism, is to be seen in the discussion of class. The concept of class is not only fundamental in Marx's social theory, and indeed, in a crucial sense, its starting point (with Marx's recognition of the proletariat as the 'revolutionary subject' in modern society, the bearer of an ideal of emancipation in the real world); it also became, as Ossowski remarked, 'the symbol of his whole doctrine and of the political programme that is derived from it'.[10] The Frankfurt School doctrine, on the other hand, has been described as 'Marxism without the proletariat';[11] and more generally, 'Western Marxism' is seen by some writers as being, at least in part, a 'philosophical meditation' on the defeats sustained by the working class in the twentieth century, particularly in the Central European revolutions that followed the First World War, and subsequently in the struggle against fascism.[12]

This theme of the decline or 'disappearance' of the working class as a revolutionary force has persisted in neo-critical theory. Thus Habermas, in *Theory and Practice*, argues that 'the proletariat *as* proletariat, has been dissolved', for while the mass of the population is proletarian in terms of its role in the process of production this situation 'is no longer bound up to such an extent with deprivation of social rewards ... and any class consciousness, especially a revolutionary class consciousness, is not to be found in the main strata of the working class today ... thus today Marx would have to abandon his hope that theory can become a material force, once it has taken hold of the masses' (pp. 196–7). Offe has expounded a similar view, in various writings. More recently Habermas has perhaps modified his conception to some extent, by referring (as I noted above, p. 64) to a 'temporarily suppressed, but unresolved class antagonism', although in a still more recent response to an essay by Agnes Heller he asserts again that we are separated from Marx by 'evident historical truths, for example that in the developed capitalist societies there is no identifiable class, no clearly circums-cribed social group which could be singled out as the representative of a general interest that has been violated'.[13]

It is a surprising feature of the judgements made about class, both by the Frankfurt School in its mature phase and by the neo-critical theorists, that they are unsupported by any analysis of the class structure or of the historical development of classes, and appear to rest only upon some kind of commonsense knowledge or 'conventional wisdom' (or as Habermas says, 'evident truths'). But serious historical and sociological analysis reveals a much more complex and ambiguous situation. If, for example, we consider the development of working class movements and parties in the Western capitalist world over the past hundred years it cannot be said that in any country, or at any time, a majority of the working class was consistently and firmly socialist (still less revolutionary) in its out-look or actions. Yet it can be argued that it has become *more* rather than less socialist in the course of the twentieth century, and espe-cially since 1945, at least until the last decade.[14] The Frankfurt School conception of the decline or disappearance of the working class as a political force seems to be based mainly upon a Utopian and millenial idea of 'revolution' which is by no means the only – or most Marxist – way of conceiving the process of social revolution, and perhaps also upon the reflection in their thought (especially in Marcuse's case) of the experience of American 'exceptionalism' – the long absence from American society of a politically organized working class.[15]

Any assessment of the present, or recent, situation of the work-ing class in advanced capitalism requires, moreover, an analysis of the whole class structure and its changes, which the Frankfurt School and neo-critical theory have signally failed to produce, or even venture upon. In this field Marxist and other radical sociologists have undertaken major studies in recent years,[16] concerned with the nature of the dominant class in advanced capitalist societies, the significance of the 'new middle classes', and the consequences of the changing social and economic position of the working class. Many controversies still rage – about the importance of the ownership of capital (and in particular its concentration in giant multinational corporations) in relation to the power of technocrats and bureaucrats; about the political orientations of the middle class; and about the emergence of a 'new working class',[17] or an entirely new class structure[18] – but all the participants recognize the continuing vigour of class conflict, and many of them assign a major historical influence to economic crises (such as that which we are currently experiencing), in a way which is quite foreign to the ideas and main concerns of critical theory.

The Frankfurt School, in its original form, and as a school of Marxism or sociology, is dead. Over the past two decades the development of Marxist thought in the social sciences, and notably in anthropology, economics and sociology, has taken a course which brings it closer to the central concerns of Marx's own theory: the analysis of modes of production, structural contradictions and historical transformations, class structure and conflict, political power and the role of the state. In the same period, and to some extent because Marxism has now established itself as one of the major paradigms in sociology, a substantial part of sociological theory and research has come to be directed upon similar issues, while the preoccupation with culture which characterized the work of Adorno and Horkheimer has diminished.[19] It is evident also that some of the principal recent studies of culture and ideology have analysed these phenomena from a theoretical standpoint profoundly different from that of the Frankfurt School; and for the most part in a structuralist framework which emphasizes their role as elements in a general process of social reproduction.[20]

But in the neo-critical theory of Habermas there is, as I have indicated, a certain *rapprochement* with both Marxism and sociology, while at the same time some of the distinctive ideas of the Frankfurt School are conserved and developed. The most prominent of these ideas, and indeed the one which has been generally regarded as constituting the basic intention of Habermas's thought, is that of 'critical theory' itself, and its location 'between philosophy and science'. In his early writings Habermas contributed to the Frankfurt School critique of positivism, but even at that time his conceptions differed significantly from those of Adorno, Horkheimer and Marcuse, in being less totally hostile to science and technology,[21] and in disregarding (or tacitly rejecting) their claim that philosophy, or art, is a form of knowledge superior to science. Subsequently, Habermas has assigned a manifestly greater importance to science, and a steadily diminishing role to philosophy. In his most recent work he argues that 'philosophy can no longer relate to the world as a whole – to nature, history, society – as a totalising knowledge'; the basic theme of philosophy – 'reason' – has now to be explored within the theoretical framework of sociology, as 'rationality'.[22]

There is an unmistakable development in Habermas's thought away from the Hegelianism of the Frankfurt School towards some kind of neo-Kantianism.[23] This is most apparent in the distinction which he now makes between the *truth* claims that we raise in empirical statements (i.e. in the sphere of theoretical reason) and the claims of *rightness* or appropriateness that we advance with norms of action and evaluation (i.e. in the sphere of practical reason). To be sure, Habermas attempts to unify these two spheres through his discourse theory of truth, but as I have argued above (pp. 60–1) there are serious objections to that theory; and the aim which he wants to achieve – namely, to establish that normative judgements are not simply matters of arbitrary decision, but are accessible, like empirical judgements, to rational argument – can be attained, or at least approached, in other ways. At the same time, Habermas's discourse theory obscures important differences between the operations of theoretical and practical reason. It is one thing to determine the structure of the DNA molecule, or of the atomic nucleus, quite another to decide what emancipation consists in; and we are merely led astray in our thinking if we do not acknowledge, and try to comprehend more fully, the differences between these two spheres of human reason with respect to the scope, conditions and outcomes of rational argument in each of them.

This is not at all intended to imply that there is one absolutely pre-eminent form of knowledge, which can supplant, or decide the validity of, other forms. Keat has demonstrated clearly that 'neither scientism nor the positivist view of science entail the possibility of a scientific politics', and further, that 'proponents of the positivist conception of science who reject the possibility of a scientific politics need not regard politics as inherently non-rational, since they may accept that science is not the only form of human knowledge or rational enquiry'.[24] Similarly, from the standpoint of scientific realism, Bhaskar has argued that 'science, although it can and must illuminate, cannot finally "settle" questions of practical morality and action, just because there are always – and necessarily – social practices besides science, and values other than cognitive ones'.[25] It makes for greater clarity, I consider, to distinguish in this way between different forms of knowledge and rational enquiry, or different social practices and values; and it is especially illuminating to separate, in Habermas's thought, two distinct elements: an empirical theory of society and a social or moral theory, which may also be called (in no pejorative sense) a social philosophy.

The latter element has so far been clearly predominant, in Habermas's discussions of communicative action and the 'emancipatory interest', as well as in his sustained argument that present-day questions of social policy have to be seen as issues for public political debate, not as 'technical' problems, arising out of a necessary evolution of society, which can be resolved by 'experts' in social science; and it has undoubtedly been the most influential aspect of his thought so far, extending far beyond the social sciences. One example of this is the attention that it has gained among theologians engaged with 'political theology' or the 'theology of liberation'. Davis, in his *Theology and Political Society*, draws substantially upon critical theory, and upon Habermas's work in particular, in discussing the questions of whether a religious tradition is an important source of experience to which an emancipatory critique may appeal, and whether the conception of communicative action as resting upon a normative foundation, itself needs to be theologically grounded.[26] Elsewhere he disputes Habermas's claim to provide a rational grounding of freedom in argumentative discourse, arguing that this is 'an exaggeration of the function and meaning of theoretical reason', and that argumentation 'can be neither the chief means nor the chief grounds of a rational consensus on freedom' (p. 95).

If Marxism is seen primarily or exclusively, as a critique of capitalist society, then clearly it is, or contains the elements of, a moral theory, in the specific form of a theory of the emancipation of the working class and the advent of a classless society. The general question of what kind of moral theory it is, and how it is grounded, has been the subject of a growing discussion, especially among the 'political theologians',[27] and although the answers proffered vary widely – and are divided particularly by the view that is taken of the relation between fact and value – they all recognize a close connection between Marxism as morality and Marxism as social science.

For those who conceive Marxism as critique, indeed, the rightness of normative judgements, or the very character of Marxism as a moral theory, may be held to depend upon its truth as science, as Turner proposes (see note [27]). It is in this context that we have to consider the most recent attempt by Habermas to formulate a theory of society, and the relation of that theory to sociology.

The view of the nature and tasks of a critical theory of society which Habermas sets out in the concluding chapter of *Theorie des kommunikativen Handelns* begins by substituting for Marx's value theory, and his analyses of capitalist society in terms of the self-expansion of capital, a concept of the social system undergoing increasing differentiation, as the basis of a theory of 'capitalist modernization'. This new theory, however, remains close to Marxism, according to Habermas because it is (like Marx's theory) *critical*, both of the contemporary social sciences and of the social reality which it attempts to grasp. Habermas then goes on to distinguish three principal research orientations in current studies of modern societies: (i) a comparative, typological, socio-historical approach, deriving largely from Max Weber, but to some extent also from Marxist historiography (for example, in the work of C. Wright Mills and Barrington Moore); (ii) a systems theory approach, which in the work of Parsons (and of Luhmann in Germany) analyses modern societies from a functionalist standpoint in terms of increasing complexity; and (iii) a theory of action, influenced by phenomenology, hermeneutics and symbolic interactionism, in which the central concerns are the 'understanding' or interpretation of images of the world and of forms of life, or more generally a 'theory of everyday life'.

By contrast with these three orientations, and after a brief review of the historical development of critical theory, Habermas adopts a research strategy which he calls 'genetic structuralism' (as an alternative to the philosophy of history of the earlier Frankfurt School). This approach is clearly influenced by the ideas of Piaget,[28] and it appears quite similar to the genetic structuralism which Goldmann expounded as a method and exemplified in his studies;[29] but since Habermas does not refer to Goldmann's work at all it is difficult to determine, without embarking on a comprehensive comparison, where the similarities and differences might lie. At all events, Habermas, after defining his approach in this way, proceeds to distinguish as the two principal forms of the rationalization of modern societies, *organized capitalism* and *bureaucratic socialism*.

The analysis of bureaucratic socialism is not pursued further, and in dealing with the development of organized capitalism Habermas largely confines himself to summarizing the conceptions which he expounded in earlier writings on the crisis tendencies in advanced capitalism. One theme, however, which is treated more fully here (Vol. II, pp. 576–83) is that of the new social conflicts that have emerged in these societies during the past two decades. Habermas notes that alongside, or in place of, institutionalized conflicts over material interests (i.e. in a broad sense, class conflicts) other conflicts have appeared, animated by new social movements, which centre upon the 'quality of life', human rights, ecological issues, equal opportunities for individual development and for participation in social decision-making. But neither the relation of these movements to older forms of political action (and in particular to the labour movement and class conflict), nor the character, growth and significance of the new social movements themselves, are subjected to any fundamental analysis or study of the kind that has been undertaken, for example, in the work of Touraine and his co-researchers.[30] It may be added that in spite of the efforts of the Starnberg Institute, the research strategy outlined by Habermas has not in fact resulted in any major empirical studies, as more Marxist or more sociological approaches have done.[31]

Habermas's overriding concern remains that of discovering some point of conjunction between philosophy and sociology, where philosophy can provide the normative grounding of a critical theory. It is this concern which determines his choice of 'rationalization' as the focus of his analysis of modern societies, for the underlying concept of rationality allows him to connect the process of rationalization with a philosophical analysis of 'reason' as embedded in language-use and communicative action; in this way, he claims, 'The social sciences can enter into a cooperative relationship with a philosophy which assumes the task of contributing to a theory of rationality' (vol. II, p. 584). This philosophy, however, is not a 'first philosophy'; its statements, like those of science, are hypothetical, and subject in some indirect way to empirical confirmation, or may enter into empirical theories (p. 587). And he concludes by suggesting that the concept of communicative action is similar to, and subsumes, Marx's concept of 'abstract labour' as the fundamental concept of an empirical science (pp. 591–3).

Thus in spite of Habermas's desire to retain philosophy as an integral component of the theory of society its role does in fact steadily diminish, and there is an increasing emphasis upon the construction of an empirical science. But this science is still very different from sociology, and in particular from Marxist sociology; and this is so for two main reasons which I discussed earlier. First, Habermas's theory of society remains largely unhistorical; it is concerned above all with the analysis and critique of modern societies, and unlike Marxism it does not set this analysis within a theory of history which undertakes to explain *all* the forms of human society and their transformations. Second, it neglects economic analysis, and indeed, as I have indicated, wants to subsume the concept of labour under that of communicative action. By contrast, it is the most distinctive feature of Marx's theory, and its most important contribution to a realistic science of society, that it does *not* deal with social interaction in general, but treats the human relation to nature, and the interaction among human beings in the production process, as determining – in the sense of setting limits to, and engendering dominant tendencies in – other forms of interaction. It is this conception which has endowed Marxism with its explanatory power, and still does so today; for whatever reconstructions of Marxist theory are needed in order to comprehend adequately the most recent stages in the development of modern societies – and in particular the role of the state and the nature of class struggles – it is still necessary to start from an analysis of the organization and control of production, whether this takes the form of the domination of capital concentrated in national or multinational corporations, or of domination through the bureaucratic management of socialized industry.

The tasks of a Marxist sociology, as I conceive it, are therefore very different from those of a neo-critical theory of society. In broad terms they involve on one side a systematic study of the course of development of 'organized capitalism' during the period since Hilferding first defined this conception in the 1920s (and this embraces investigations of the changing organization of production, the diverse forms of state intervention, and changes in class relations); on the other side, an analysis of the forms of organization of production, and their consequences, in the socialist countries, as well as a study of the social and historical conditions which made possible the emergence of Bolshevism as a distorted form of Marxist thought. Much of this research is, of course, already being undertaken by Marxists of various persuasions; and its most general characteristic is that it concentrates upon those two spheres of enquiry – the economy and social history – which have been sadly neglected by the Frankfurt School and by neo-critical theory.

NOTES

[1]   Karl Korsch, *Marxism and Philosophy* (1923; English translation London, New Left Books, 1970), p. 42. Korsch, however, unlike the Frankfurt School thinkers, later changed his view and came to regard the elaboration of Marxism in the form of a general social philosophy as a 'distortion'; 'The main tendency of historical materialism', he concluded, 'is no longer "philosophical", but is that of an empirical scientific method', *Karl Marx* (rev. German edn, Frankfurt, Europäische Verlagsanstalt, 1967), p. 203.

[2]   On the problems of a Marxist analysis of different forms of society and their transformations see the entries in Tom Bottomore (ed.), *A Dictionary of Marxist Thought* (Oxford, Blackwell, 1983), on 'Ancient society', 'Asiatic society', 'Feudal society', 'Transition from feudalism to capitalism'. See also the two studies by Perry Anderson, *Passages from Antiquity to Feudalism* (London, New Left Books, 1974), and *Lineages of the Absolutist State* (London, New Left Books, 1974); Lawrence Krader, *The Asiatic Mode of Production* (Assen, Van Goreum, 1975); Bryan S. Turner, *Marx and the End of Orientalism* (London, Allen & Unwin, 1978); as well as the recent analyses of tribal societies by Marxist anthropologists, which are reviewed in David Seddon (ed.), *Relations of Production* (London, Frank Cass, 1978), 'Marxism and Anthropology: A Preliminary Survey'.

[3]   Fernand Braudel, *Civilization and Capitalism, 15th–18th Century* (3 vols, 1979; English translation, London, Collins, and New York, Harper & Row, 1981–1983).

[4]   The discussion began with an article by R. Brenner, 'Agrarian Class Structure and Economic Development in Pre-Industrial Europe', *Past and Present*, no. 70 (1976), continued in nos 78, 79, 80 (1978) and no. 85 (1979), and concluded with a rejoinder by Brenner, 'The Agrarian Roots of European Capitalism' in no. 97 (1982).

[5]   Henryk Grossmann, *Das Akkumulations- und Zusammenbruchsgesetz des kapitalistischen Systems* (1929; new edn, Frankfurt, Neue Kritik, 1967).

[6]   Jay, *The Dialectical Imagination* (Boston, Little, Brown & Co., 1973), pp. 16–17.

[7]   Rudolf Hilferding, *Finance Capital* (1910; English translation London, Routledge & Kegan Paul, 1981). My introduction to

the translation gives an account of Hilferding's essays of the 1920s on 'organized capitalism'; see also Hilferding, 'The Organized Economy', in Tom Bottomore and Patrick Goode (eds.), *Readings in Marxist Sociology* (Oxford, Oxford University Press, 1983), pp. 247–53).

[8] Franz Neumann, *Behemoth* (New York, Oxford University Press, 1944).

[9] For example, the studies by Henryk Grossmann and Franz Neumann, already mentioned, and by Ernest Mandel and Paul Sweezy.

[10] Stanislaw Ossowski, *Class Structure in the Social Consciousness* (London, Routledge & Kegan Paul, 1963), p. 71.

[11] Leszek Kolakowski, *Main Currents of Marxism* (Oxford, Oxford University Press, 1968), vol. III, pp. 357–415.

[12] See the entry 'Western Marxism', in Tom Bottomore (ed.), *A Dictionary of Marxist Thought*; and also Perry Anderson, *Considerations on Western Marxism* (London, New Left Books, 1976).

[13] In Thompson and Held (eds.), *Habermas: Critical Debates*, p. 221.

[14] I have discussed this question at greater length in an essay on 'The Political Role of the Working Class in Western Europe', in Tom Bottomore, *Sociology and Socialism* (Brighton, Harvester Press, 1984). It is important to note here that there are considerable differences between countries, and also major historical fluctuations, which can only be properly assessed by the kind of comparative sociological study that the Frankfurt School eschewed.

[15] On this subject see the introduction by C. T. Husbands to the English translation of Werner Sombart, *Why is there no Socialism in the United States?* (London, Macmillan, 1976), and various essays in John Laslett and S. M. Lipset (eds), *Failure of a Dream? Essays in the History of American Socialism* (Garden City, New York, Anchor/Doubleday, 1967).

[16] See, for example, Harry Braverman, *Labor and Monopoly Capital* (New York, Monthly Review Press, 1974); Nicos Poulantzas, *Classes in Contemporary Capitalism* (London, New Left Books, 1975); Alain Touraine, *The Post-Industrial Society* (New York, Random House, 1971) and *The Self-Production of Society* (Chicago, University of Chicago Press, 1977); Erik Olin Wright, *Class, Crisis and the State* (London, New Left Books, 1978).

[17] See Serge Mallet, *The New Working Class* (Nottingham,

Spokesman Books, 1975); and for a concise, critical survey of some of the principal views, Michael Mann, *Consciousness and Action Among the Western Working Class* (London, Macmillan, 1973).

[18]   Argued particularly by Touraine in *The Post-Industrial Society*, and in later writings which emphasize the role of the new social movements.

[19]   It is difficult, of course, to define precisely the main theoretical orientations of the present time or recent past in a discipline so diverse and changing as sociology, but some indications may be gained from a collection of papers initiated by the Research Council of the International Sociological Association; see Tom Bottomore, Stefan Nowak, and Magdalena Sokolowska (eds), *Sociology: The State of the Art* (London and Beverly Hills, Sage Publications, 1982).

[20]   See, as one important example of a different approach, Pierre Bourdieu and Jean-Claude Passeron, *Reproduction in Education, Society and Culture* (London and Beverly Hills, Sage Publications, 1977); and on the Marxist theory of ideology more generally, Jorge Larrain, *Marxism and Ideology* (London, Macmillan, 1983) which examines the development of the theory from Marx to Gramsci, discusses Althusser and structuralism, and ignores the Frankfurt School, though devoting some critical pages to Habermas's theory of language and communication.

[21]   See especially his essay, 'Technology and Science as "Ideology"' (1968), in *Toward a Rational Society* (Boston, Beacon Press, 1970), in which he rejects Marcuse's ideas of a 'new science' based upon a 'hermeneutics of nature'. This essay is a clear and succinct exposition of Habermas's fundamental conceptions, which are developed at much greater length in his later work, and provides an accessible introduction to his thought.

[22]   *Theorie des kommunikativen Handelns* (2 vols, Frankfurt, Suhrkamp, 1981), pp. 15–24. See also my discussion of this work on p. 61 above.

[23]   And perhaps towards a view which would be compatible with scientific realism; but Habermas has not yet engaged in any discussion of this more recent philosophy of science.

[24]   Russell Keat, *The Politics of Social Theory* (Oxford, Blackwell, 1981), p. 21.

[25]   Roy Bhaskar, *The Possibility of Naturalism*, pp. 82–3.

[26]   Charles Davis, *Theology and Political Society* (Cambridge, Cam-

bridge University Press, 1980), especially chaps. 5 and 6. Davis also draws attention to the extensive discussion in Germany, notably in the writings of J. B. Metz and H. Peukert.

[27] See especially Denys Turner, *Marxism and Christianity* (Oxford, Blackwell, 1983) who argues that 'Marxism, as the critical science of bourgeois society and ideology, is – if indeed it is truly 'scientific' – all that we could expect morality to be under bourgeois conditions' (p. 83). See also the discussion, from a different perspective, in the forthcoming book by Steven Lukes, *Marxism and Morality*. Some earlier discussions are also still relevant, and in particular those by the Austro-Marxists; e.g. Otto Bauer, 'Marxism and Ethics' (translated in Bottomore and Goode, *Austro-Marxism* (Oxford, Oxford University Press, 1978), pp. 78–84), and Max Adler, 'Ethik und Wissenschaft' and 'Marxismus und Ethik', in *Marxistische Probleme* (Stuttgart, J. H. W. Dietz, 1913).

[28] See Jean Piaget, *Structuralism* (New York, Basic Books, 1970).

[29] See especially Lucien Goldmann, 'Genèse et structure' in *Marxisme et sciences humaines* (Paris, Gallimard, 1970), and *Towards a Sociology of the Novel* (London, Tavistock Publications, 1975).

[30] See Alain Touraine, *The Self-Production of Society* (Chicago, University of Chicago Press, 1977); also the studies of particular movements – the student movement, women's movement, anti-nuclear movement, regional nationalist movements – initiated by Touraine, and the volume of debates, Alain Touraine (ed.), *Mouvements sociaux d'aujourd'hui: acteurs et analystes* (Paris, Éditions ouvrières, 1982).

[31] See the brief note on the Institute's research projects by Thomas McCarthy in his Introduction to *Legitimation Crisis* (London, Heinemann, 1976), pp. viii, 144.

Biographical Notes on Some Leading Members of the School

Theodor W. Adorno (1903–1969) After studying philosophy, sociology, psychology and music at the University of Frankfurt, Adorno went to Vienna in 1925, where he studied composition for three years with Alban Berg and participated in the musical discussions of the Schönberg circle. Returning to Frankfurt he became a *Privatdozent* in the University in 1931 and began an informal association with the Institute of Social Research. After the Nazi seizure of power he spent the next four years studying at Merton College, Oxford, before moving to New York and becoming a full member of the Institute (1938). In the USA Adorno continued his philosophical writings and studies of music, and also participated in a project on studies of prejudice and authoritarianism which resulted in a major collective work, *The Authoritarian Personality*. When the Institute returned to Frankfurt in 1950 Adorno became assistant director, then co-director and finally, after the retirement of Horkheimer and Pollock in 1959, director.

Adorno's principal writings available in English are: *Minima Moralia* (London, New Left Books, 1974), *Negative Dialectics* (New York, Seabury Press, 1973), *Philosophy of Modern Music* (New York, Seabury Press, 1973), *Prisms* (London, Neville Spearman, 1969);

and (with Horkheimer) *Dialectic of Enlightenment* (New York, Herder and Herder, 1972), (with others) *The Authoritarian Personality* (New York, Harper & Row, 1950).

Jürgen Habermas (b. 1929) The major thinker of the late or post-Frankfurt School, Habermas studied with Adorno and became his assistant, taught philosophy at Heidelberg, then became professor of philosophy and sociology at Frankfurt before moving (in 1972) to the Max-Planck Institute in Starnberg. Recently he has returned to the University of Frankfurt as a professor. His principal writings, mainly concerned with problems of the theory of knowledge, but more recently also with Marx's theory of history and with the analysis of late capitalist society, are: *Towards a Rational Society* (London, Heinemann, 1970), *Knowledge and Human Interests* (London, Heinemann, 1971), *Legitimation Crisis* (London, Heinemann, 1976), *Communication and the Evolution of Society* (London, Heinemann, 1979).

Max Horkheimer (1895–1971) After a commercial training, at the urging of his father (a prominent manufacturer), Horkheimer turned to academic studies, first in psychology, then in philosophy. He became *Privatdozent* at the University of Frankfurt in 1925, and was one of the earliest members (together with his lifelong friend, Friedrich Pollock) of the Institute, of which he became the second director in 1931, having already been appointed to a newly created chair of social philosophy in the University in 1929. After the Nazi seizure of power Horkheimer moved first to Geneva and then, in 1934, to New York when the Institute found a home on the campus of Columbia University. Horkheimer returned with the Institute to Frankfurt in 1950 and continued as director until his retirement in 1959. His principal writings are: *Critical Theory: Selected Essays* (New York, Herder and Herder, 1972), *Eclipse of Reason* (New York, Oxford University Press, 1947; reprinted Seabury Press, 1974), and (with Adorno) *Dialectic of Enlightenment* (New York, Herder and Herder, 1972).

Herbert Marcuse (1898–1979) Studied philosophy at the Universities of Berlin and Freiburg (at the latter with Husserl and Heidegger), and became a member of the Institute in 1932. In 1933 he moved, with other members, to Geneva and then to New York where he worked with Horkheimer in the Institute from 1934 to 1940. He then served in the Eastern European section of the US State Department until 1950, when he returned to Columbia, taught at Brandeis

University from 1954 to 1967, and thereafter at the University of California. His major writings are: *Reason and Revolution: Hegel and the Rise of Social Theory* (New York, Oxford University Press, 1941), *Eros and Civilization: A Philosophical Inquiry into Freud* (Boston, Beacon Press, 1951), *Soviet Marxism: A Critical Analysis* (New York, Columbia University Press, 1958), *One-Dimensional Man* (Boston, Beacon Press, 1964), and a volume of articles from the 1930s, *Negations: Essays in Critical Theory* (Boston, Beacon Press, 1968).

Friedrich Pollock (1894–1970) He was trained for a commercial career, but after the First World War became a student of economics and politics at the universities of Munich, Freiburg and Frankfurt. He took part in the 'First Marxist Work Week' organized by his friend Felix Weil in 1923, and was a leading member of the Institute from its foundation. A lifelong close friend of Horkheimer, Pollock moved with him to New York, and then returned to Frankfurt in 1950. When they retired in 1959 Pollock and Horkheimer moved to adjoining villas in Montagnola, Switzerland. Pollock published a study of Soviet planning (in German, 1929), a number of essays in the 1930s and 1940s now collected under the title *The Stages of Capitalism* (in German, 1975), and *The Economic and Social Consequences of Automation* (Oxford, Oxford University Press, 1957).

Suggestions for Further Reading

The Frankfurt School has been passionately supported and equally passionately attacked. Two major, very sympathetic (though not uncritical) accounts of the school are Martin Jay, *The Dialectical Imagination: A History of the Frankfurt School and the Institute of Social Research, 1923–1950* (Boston, Little, Brown & Co., 1973), and David Held, *Introduction to Critical Theory: Horkheimer to Habermas* (London, Hutchinson, 1980).

More critical accounts are to be found in Leszek Kolakowski, *Main Currents of Marxism* (Oxford, Oxford University Press, 1978), Vol. III, Chapters X and XI; Zolton Tar, *The Frankfurt School: The Critical Theories of Max Horkheimer and Theodor W. Adorno* (New York, Wiley & Sons, 1977); George Lichtheim, 'From Marx to Hegel', in *From Marx to Hegel and other Essays* (London, Orbach and Chambers, 1971); and briefly, as part of a general criticism of 'Western Marxism', in Perry Anderson, *Considerations on Western Marxism* (London, New Left Books, 1976).

The work of some individual members of the school has also been discussed in more sympathetic or more critical vein. On Adorno see Susan Buck-Morss, *The Origin of Negative Dialectics; Theodor W. Adorno, Walter Benjamin and the Frankfurt Institute* (Brighton, Harvester Press, 1977), and Gillian Rose, *The Melancholy Science: An Introduction to the Thought of Theodor W. Adorno* (London, Macmillan,

1978) – both generally sympathetic and to be compared with the very critical assessment by Kolakowski mentioned above. Marcuse is discussed in a highly critical manner in Alasdair MacIntyre, *Marcuse* (London, Fontana/Collins, 1970); but there is as yet no major separate assessment in English of Horkheimer's work. An important study of Habermas is Thomas McCarthy, *The Critical Theory of Jürgen Habermas* (Cambridge, Mass., MIT Press, 1978), while a more critical evaluation is presented in Russell Keat, *The Politics of Social Theory: Habermas, Freud and the Critique of Positivism* (Oxford, Blackwell, 1981).

The principal writings of leading members of the Frankfurt School are listed in the *Biographical Notes* (see previous section). However, there are also some useful collections of excerpts from their writings, with commentaries and evaluations; see especially, Andrew Arato and Eike Gebhardt (eds), *The Essential Frankfurt School Reader* (New York, Urizen Books, 1978), and Paul Connerton (ed.), *Critical Sociology: Selected Readings* (Harmondsworth, Penguin Books, 1976).

Index